THE COMEBACK

THE COMEBACK

— HOW —

TODAY'S MOMS

REENTER THE

WORKPLACE

SUCCESSFULLY

CHERYL CASONE
WITH STEPHANIE KRIKORIAN

PORTFOLIO/PENGUIN

PORTFOLIO/PENGUIN

An imprint of Penguin Random House LLC
375 Hudson Street
New York, New York 10014

ISBN: 978-1-101-97982-2
E-book ISBN: 978-1-101-97984-6

Printed in the United States of America
1   3   5   7   9   10   8   6   4   2

Book design by Alissa Rose Theodor

To working mothers everywhere

— CONTENTS —

Many of the names in this book have been changed to protect the privacy of the women who so generously offered to be a part of this project.

— FOREWORD —

I was lucky to grow up with a mom who told me every night before she put me to bed that I could be anything I wanted to be. I believed her, knowing full well that achieving my goals would require a lot of hard work.

I had big dreams, and I achieved many of them. I was a child concert violinist, high school valedictorian, a student at Stanford, and winner of the Miss America pageant in 1989. I parlayed those experiences and discipline into twenty-five years in the television business: working my way up the ranks from cub reporter in Richmond, Virginia, to Cincinnati, Cleveland, Dallas, and finally to New York City and hosting my own show on Fox News.

Along the way, I remembered my mom's words—that I could be anything I wanted to be, and as a child I didn't see any challenges to that truth. But as I grew older, I learned that the workplace can be cruel to women and that none of us will succeed if we don't say yes to our dreams, no to self-imposed guilt, and help each other.

I faced sexual harassment early on in my career, both as Miss America and in my television work. Stereotypes preceded me at every new job. "Here comes the former Miss America bimbo," they'd say. After being fired from my anchor job in Cleveland, Ohio, one week after getting married, I was told I'd be fine "now that I had a husband." I had to work triply hard to dispel all negativity, always pushing myself forward to fulfill my dream of being the best reporter in the shop, and I know many women have to work harder than I did to overcome worse obstacles.

As if the world wasn't harsh enough, many of us women impose further burdens on ourselves. We try to have it all. Stay-at-home moms feel guilty for not having high-powered careers. Working moms feel guilty for leaving their children at home. Guilt seems to be an acceptable mode for mothers no matter what they do.

It's time for that to end. If you're a mom considering reentering the workplace, don't waste time on guilt. Instead, be clear in your own mind and heart about what kind of person you want to be and what kind of parent you want to be. The choice to return to your career is a very personal choice, and no one can tell you what you ought to do.

Whatever you choose, there will be trade-offs. I personally always knew I wanted to be a mom with a career, and I aspire to be an example to my children of a fulfilled human being. To be that example, I have to be realistic. Being a mom is my most important role, but it's not my *only* role. So, even though I'm a person who likes to give 100 percent to everything I do, I have learned that I can only give 100 percent to what I'm doing *in the moment*. If I'm at work, am I giving 100 percent to my kids? No. If I'm at home, am I giving 100 percent to my work? No. But I'm 100 percent wherever I am at the moment. It's a balancing act, but worthwhile as long as we don't kid ourselves that we're superwomen.

Since we aren't superwomen, we need help. Being a working mom is much easier with a supportive partner who understands your life goals, too, and shares the responsibilities for raising children. I let my future husband know I wanted to be a working mom from the beginning of our relationship, and I'm glad I did. And let's face it. Even when women lay out the ground rules and hope for 50/50, it doesn't really ever happen that way very often. Still, it's better to start that way and continue to work together as a team with the goal of both feeling fulfilled.

One of the most important lessons I've learned from almost three decades in the business is that I've decided that I choose to work outside the home more for my eleven-year-old son than for my thirteen-year-old daughter, because I believe we must continue to change the way men—especially younger men—think and feel about women in powerful roles. My hope is that by watching me, my son will have the same amount of respect and admiration for his eventual female colleagues as he currently has for his mom. If women are to make it over the hurdles currently placed before them in the workplace, we will need to raise a generation of *men helping women.*

Women must also help women. I've been fortunate in my career to have had several strong female bosses who challenged me to step into roles I wasn't just quite ready for yet and inspired me to be the best I could be. I've also had women who deliberately tried to take me down just because. After I was crowned Miss America, a well-known television reporter in New York tried to make a mockery of my accomplishment by asking me a series of questions so inappropriate ("Have you ever done drugs?" And "Have you ever had sex?") that the entire press corps actually booed her. The vast differences in the experiences I've had is why I've made it one of my life missions to make sure I give back, always conscious of empowering other women along the way.

Cheryl Casone is one of the strong professional women who empower others, and she has written *The Comeback* to join in that effort to help other women reach their goals—and feed their families. As a fellow journalist, I can say that Cheryl's vision and methodology have produced an excellent book. As a working mom, I can say that the book is not only excellent, but indispensable, a must-read for all the brave mothers looking to make a comeback.

Making a comeback takes courage, as I learned from my own mother who after encouraging me to follow my dreams was able to follow her own. For forty years she dedicated her life to raising her children, but in the last ten years she's been the CEO of our family car dealership business. During that time, it almost all went away. My parents were stripped of a dealership that had been in our family for almost one hundred years when General Motors and the government shuttered dealerships all across the country. Turns out, there wasn't any real reason for my parents to lose their livelihood. Main Motor Sales in Anoka, Minnesota, was still a profitable business and one of the top sellers of trucks in the entire state. My mom decided she was not going to allow a privately owned company to be taken away without a fight. She lobbied every member of Congress in our state and even went to Capitol Hill to make her voice heard, and guess what? She got the business back.

I'm grateful that my mom made the comeback, and I hope more women have the courage to follow their dreams. Challenge yourself to be one of them, and if that means getting back into the workforce or starting your own business, know that I am cheering you from the sidelines and saying exactly what my mom still tells me today: "You can be anything you want to be." I believe in comebacks and I certainly believe you will be inspired by Cheryl's book.

Gretchen Carlson, host of *The Real Story with Gretchen Carlson*
on the Fox News Channel, author of *Getting Real*

THE COMEBACK

— INTRODUCTION —

Marsha, a secretary, had always worked full time before she became a mom. She took two years off when she had a baby girl and then, when she went back to work, chose temping so that she could spend more time with her daughter. Marsha wanted to be able to stay home when her baby was sick or when she and her husband wanted to take a vacation, and temp work gave her that flexibility while allowing her to keep her job skills and business contacts up to date.

Her daughter, an only child, went to day care and did well there. She liked having kids to play with and, luckily, was a very easy child at home. When her daughter turned four and was gearing up for kindergarten, Marsha knew it was time to go back to work full time. She loved being home with her daughter but, in truth, she loved working, too: "It rounded out my life." Working was what she knew—going to an office, meeting goals, and experiencing adult social interaction. It was something she really liked and needed as part of her life. Staying at home full time, especially with a happy and healthy child in school, just wasn't for her.

It's possible she could also see the writing on the wall, for not long after returning to work, she and her husband separated, and later divorced.

Marsha is in her seventies now, but she remembers her days as a working mom with great pride. Working made her whole and satisfied. It made her happy, and that made her a happy mother. She still thinks that mothers who work outside the home get the best of both worlds, despite the sacrifices and challenges they face. Marsha had only a few professional options in her era—secretary, teacher, and maybe nurse. That's changed today, of course, but still she believes that she and other moms like her set a good example for their children by working outside the home.

She's right—her child was positively affected and influenced by her decision to work. I should know. I'm that child. Every morning, I watched my mother get up early to prepare for her day and help me get ready for mine before we headed out the door together. Every night I felt her enthusiasm and love when she got home and spent the evening with me. And on weekends it was just the two of us, too. I never felt her absence. She was always there for me and I'm a better person for having witnessed and lived her warmth and work ethic. She was my role model: a hardworking career woman who, in my eyes, had every-thing, and I looked up to her for her ability to juggle her life at work and home with what seemed to be great ease. I'm grateful for the stan-dard she set.

She was, in part, the inspiration for this book. As a business reporter and anchor, one of the biggest stories I have covered at Fox Business Network was the collapse of Lehman Brothers on Septem-ber 15, 2008, and the ensuing collapse of the U.S. economy. Unbe-knownst to me at the time, that event would put me in a position to talk to many women like my mom, who were doing their best to balance their responsibilities at work and at home. Many were com-ing back to work after long absences, forced to return when their husbands lost their jobs to layoffs, cutbacks, and complete corporate closures. At its worst point, unemployment in the country hit 10 percent.[1] People were desperate for information: Who was hiring? What sectors were coming out of the slump fastest? And I had the answers. I had my finger not only on the pulse of Wall Street, but also of Silicon Valley, the manufacturing sector, the entertainment industry, and many others. Suddenly, jobs became my beat.

Following the recession, I continued to do segments on jobs, and of course women in the workforce were an enormous part of that story. One day during a commercial break, Elisabeth Hasselbeck, at the time anchoring *Fox & Friends*, mentioned that she had many brilliant, creative, experienced mom-friends out there who were ready to reenter the market but were struggling to figure out how. She asked me what information I had on moms making a comeback. At the time I had none. But I promised to do some digging. And as I did, I thought about my mom. I thought about all of my colleagues and friends who had left to have babies and were now working to restart their careers. And I thought about all the other mothers, many in much more difficult situations than my friends, who were facing tough odds as they fought to support their families. I not only sympathized with these women, but I also realized we needed them in the workforce—and the seed for a book was planted.

At first I was hesitant to tackle a project that focused on mothers. I wasn't a mom and had never intended to become one. But I worked in a field populated by a lot of women, and I'd seen what happened when they left to have children and then came back. I'd witnessed how the rapid pace of technology put them at a disadvantage, and how they

---

1. "Labor Force Statistics from the Current Population Survey," Bureau of Labor Statistics, 2015, http://data.bls.gov/timeseries/LNS14000000.

struggled to figure out a new system that had been installed while they were gone until I, or one of my sympathetic colleagues, taught them what they needed to know. In other jobs before my current one at Fox, I saw moms get passed over for promotions—punished, essentially, for having taken a leave of absence, something I and my male colleagues never experienced.

But I came to realize that I had something valuable to offer. My perspective was and still is unique: I'm a woman, a reporter, and a job-and-career expert with access to leaders of industry and a view from the trenches. I'm the girl co-workers confide in and approach with questions. I'm the journalist who will dig deep to find information. And I'm a woman who advocates for other women. If my girlfriends found this combination of experience and access helpful, perhaps other women would, too.

I started my research by interviewing women I knew and then hit social media, asking moms everywhere for their perspectives. Those who connected then helped me spread the word via parenting and mom blogs in order to reach even more women. Eventually, I collected interviews with hundreds of mothers from all walks of life. I asked them about their secret sauce—how did they make things work at work? How did they land the job they wanted? How difficult was it and what mistakes did they make along the way? How did they reignite a career that had gone cold? Nobody I spoke to was short on stories—everyone had faced hurdles, taken missteps, and learned a lot. Everyone had usable and valuable tips for others. Many wished they could have a do-over.

What was most surprising and gratifying as I reported this book was how many women were excited to take the time to speak with me.

They moved me with their generosity. I'd chat with one mom and she'd eagerly suggest a friend who had experienced a different hurdle. They all wanted to help so other women could learn from their challenges, mistakes, and successes. Their enthusiasm was universal, regardless of where they lived in the country or what they did for a living. It was a nonstop train of women helping women—so absolutely refreshing it warmed my heart. I interviewed doctors and lawyers and fitness instructors and a waitress. I interviewed people on Wall Street and Main Street and everywhere in between. Teachers and journalists and military veterans and entrepreneurs and social workers—I pursued them all, soaking up their boots-on-the-ground wisdom. The common thread among them: a burning desire to succeed at work.

A large number of the mothers I spoke to had always planned to return to work, but it wasn't until they were faced with difficult circumstances or forces beyond their control, like the recession or a divorce, that they had to. But regardless of why they reentered the workforce, their experiences were all eerily similar. Corporate America is still not mom-friendly, even though mothers make up almost 50 percent of the workforce. And I discovered that there were few places for this particular group of women to turn to for support and career advice.

Once I learned about the hurdles they'd encountered, I reached out to find solutions. I interviewed employment lawyers, psychologists, financial planners, career coaches, human resources managers, and CEOs. They all offered guidance and step-by-step instruction for overcoming obstacles and getting back on the fast track at work, whatever that work may be.

I wrote this book because every woman should have the chance to succeed simultaneously at work and motherhood the way my own mother did. I wrote it because there has been a profound shift in the way we work and the speed with which things change, and whether they've been out for a while or just a few months, women need a one-stop resource to help guide them as they make their way back into the workforce. I wrote it because women need to know that they have a tremendous amount to offer to the workplace. And finally, I wrote it because women need to stick together, and those of us with access to information have a responsibility to share it with those who don't.

Each chapter is filled with anecdotes, tips, encouragement, and even some tough-love advice. You'll learn from the moms in the trenches as well as those at the top of major corporations—some of whom are moms themselves. The book covers all bases, laying the groundwork for moms thinking of taking maternity leave, for those who have just quit their jobs and need to learn how to stay connected, for those starting their search to get back into the workforce after an absence, and for those who've landed a job, advice that will enable them to go on killing it. I want you all to succeed.

There are many books offering suggestions for how to make corporate America more welcoming to mothers. There are many books offering suggestions for how to achieve work/life balance. *The Comeback* is neither. It is simply a guide to help mothers stay in control over the trajectory of their lives, and give them the tools to make a smooth reentry into the workplace should they decide they want to—or have to—go back to work. I wrote it for all the working women who might one day become moms, and all the working moms who might become stay-at-home moms or moms who start a business and work from home. No matter who you are, no matter why change comes into your life, I hope this book will help you to do what my mom did: to stare that change in the face and say with confidence, "Bring it."

Part I

Planning Your

Comeback

1

Welcome Back

Anyone who thinks being a stay-at-home mom is easy has never been one. It's a job that demands the patience of a teacher, the organizing skills of a wedding planner, the financial savvy of an accountant, and the protective instincts of a police officer. And today many stay-at-home moms have been trained in these professions. They held these jobs before they left the workforce to focus exclusively on raising their children.

Their reasons for leaving are varied: the burden of day-care costs; the fear they'll miss out on their kids' childhood; the exhaustion and stress of trying to juggle work and family; a spouse with a demanding, inflexible job, or who believes his career must take priority; or simply a deep desire to be home with their children.

With so many women bringing their professional expertise and experience home with them, it's no wonder that many of today's stay-at-home mothers make Betty Draper and June Cleaver look like amateurs. You're probably one of them. You spearheaded the fund-raisers that grew your PTA budget from $15,000 to $28,000 in two years. You can creatively stretch a healthy meal to feed four people over three days. You are an advocate for children—yours and others. You can multitask like nobody's business, and you can get more done in one day than many people get done in a week. A lot of stay-at-home mothers love being at home, and take great pride in doing the important, unpaid work that keeps the world running.

And yet for some women, this isn't enough. They miss the high-stakes work environment. They find themselves feeling claustrophobic in lives dominated by housework, playdates, and school-related activities. They miss being paid, because in our culture paid work commands respect. They miss the stimulation and the adrenaline rush of feeling like they're part of something big. They decide they want to set a different example for their children. They feel like their education was wasted, and their ambitions were left unfulfilled. They're facing an empty nest and want a new challenge. One of the most powerful statements I heard was simply this: "I didn't want to just be known as Tyler's mom."

The reasons why stay-at-home mothers return to work are intensely personal and varied—as intensely personal and varied as the reasons they chose to leave in the first place. Yet no matter how much you love raising a family, or how good you are at stay-at-home motherhood, the fact is that for better or for worse, it is highly likely that one day you will decide it's time to return to the workplace.

COMEBACK QUOTE

"Ultimately by going back to work there was an emotional payoff. I liked having my own identity. When I was around a few people that were working, I was interested to see their independence, the self-confidence that was there, because life wasn't just their kids. It wasn't just about going on vacation. It wasn't about what they were doing to decorate their house. If I had to go to one more cookout barbecue and hear someone tell me about what curtains they were

> buying or what trip they were going on . . . We couldn't afford to do
> that sort of stuff if we stayed on one income. I didn't feel a lack for
> it, so it wasn't a competition, but it was a very one-dimensional exis-
> tence."
>
> —Tina, executive search consultant, mother of two

Maybe such a change of heart seems unthinkable to you, or maybe such a change of heart still wouldn't drive you to give up your role as a stay-at-home mom. The majority of the hundreds of women I interviewed for this book felt the same way. They never thought they'd go back to work, and yet they did. Some did it for the reasons above. Some did it not because they wanted to, but because they had to. Think that couldn't happen to you? Consider these statistics:

- Approximately 40 percent of marriages end in divorce.[2]

- The projected average cost for four years of college tuition and fees at an in-state public college will be almost $95,000 by 2033.[3]

- About 31 percent of Americans have no retirement savings, no pension, no savings account, nothing.[4]

---

2. "Provisional Number of Marriages and Marriage Rate: United States, 2000–2014," Centers for Disease Control and Prevention, http://www.cdc.gov/nchs/nvss/marriage _divorce_tables.htm.

3. "Tutorial: The Real Cost of Higher Education," SavingForCollege.com, http://www.sav ingforcollege.com/tutorial101/the_real_cost_of_higher_education.php.

4. "Report on the Economic Well-Being of U.S. Households in 2014," Board of Governors of the Federal Reserve System, http://www.federalreserve.gov/econresdata/2014-report -economic-well-being-us-households-201505.pdf.

- 52 percent of working-age households—that's 46 million people—are "at risk" of being unable to maintain their preretirement standard of living in retirement.[5]

- The average age of widowhood is fifty-five years old.[6]

- Nearly 5 million women managing a household alone live below the poverty line.[7]

I hope none of you return to work because of hardship, but the odds are good that you will head back to full-time employment at some point in your life. And for some of you, maybe that time has already arrived.

If so, welcome back. Even if rejoining the workforce is not your first choice, this is going to be an exciting new chapter in your life. If your kids are grown, you're about to embark on an interesting rediscovery process. After all, you're still the intelligent, capable person you were the last time you worked for a paycheck—you've just got a heck of a lot more life experience and perspective under your belt. And if your kids are little, they're still going to be fine.

Many of the mothers I interviewed for this book expressed amazement at how well their families coped even though they weren't always

---

5. "NRRI Update Shows Half Still Falling Short," Center for Retirement Research at Boston College, December 2014. Study based on the Federal Reserve's Survey of Consumer Finances. http://crr.bc.edu/wp-content/uploads/2014/12/IB_14-20-508.pdf.

6. David A. Weaver, "Widows and Social Security," *Social Security Bulletin* 70, 3 (2010); https://www.socialsecurity.gov/policy/docs/ssb/v70n3/v70n3p89.pdf.

7. Carmen DeNavas-Walt and Bernadette D. Proctor, "Income and Poverty in the United States, 2014: Current Population Reports," United States Census Bureau, https://www.census.gov/content/dam/Census/library/publications/2015/demo/p60-252.pdf.

around during the day anymore. Several were stunned to learn that their children didn't resent them for going off to work, but rather appreciated them even more. In fact, a Harvard Business School study found that daughters of working mothers grew up to be more successful than their immediate peers. They earned more and were likely to hold management positions. And it wasn't just the daughters who benefited; boys, too, were found to be more successful if they had a working mom. Those findings don't negate all the advantages many children enjoy by having their mother at home—it just indicates that children are remarkably resilient so long as your love and support are never in doubt. And with that reassurance, many moms who made their comeback have found great satisfaction in their jobs, and a renewed sense of pride and independence.

That said, all the women I've spoken to about their experience in reentering the workplace admitted that getting to that great result wasn't easy. I get it. It's hard to return to work when women still only make roughly seventy-nine cents to every dollar a man makes in a full-time position,[8] which can make it hard to pay for child care and commuting costs. It's hard when you know your commitment to your work will be questioned, and your professional advancement hampered, if you take advantage of company-sponsored flex scheduling or family leave policies. It's hard when technology advances so fast that your knowledge might be obsolete even if you've only been out of the workforce for a year or two. And it's really, really hard to regain your

---

8. Carmen DeNavas-Walt and Bernadette D. Proctor, "Income and Poverty in the United States, 2014: Current Population Reports," United States Census Bureau, https://www.census.gov/content/dam/Census/library/publications/2015/demo/p60-252.pdf.

confidence and a sense of how valuable you are to the workplace if you've spent the last five years covered in Cheerios and baby drool, or if the bulk of your conversations during the day involved arguing unsuccessfully that mac 'n' cheese is not a food group, or when you just caught your teenagers rolling their eyes—again—at your comic attempts to figure out what the heck to do with Twitter.

It's so hard, in fact, that it explains why the number of U.S. women of working age in the labor market has grown by only one percentage point since 1990, according to the Organisation for Economic Co-operation and Development. It's so hard that more than half the women I interviewed only returned to the workforce because they had to. And therein lies the problem, because things look a lot scarier, and options are far more limited, when people don't plan ahead for curveballs and wait until they have no other choice but to make a move.

Here's the really, really good news: It doesn't actually have to be so hard. With a little planning, forethought, and even imagination, you can stay home with your children as long as you like and still be prepared to jump back into the workforce should you ever decide it's the right thing to do. It's like having insurance. You may never need it, but wouldn't it be better—for you and your family—to be prepared?

Ideally, you're a newlywed or newly pregnant, and you're planning ahead before you're ready to take your maternity leave. But if you're still juggling work and kids and starting to think the struggle and stress isn't worth it, you can still make a smooth transition out and eventually a smooth one back in, should you want or need it. If you've already left the workplace and are wondering whether you'll ever figure out how to get back, or whether it's even worth the bother: I'm telling you, you can, and it is.

Maybe you have no choice about the return—you are going back because your family needs the income. Even if that's the case, keep in mind that you may find your restarted career rewarding. The best-case scenario for moms returning to the workforce is that they find something that will complement and enrich not only their lives, but also the lives of their families. No one is one dimensional, and although it may seem daunting to consider juggling yet another ball, working at a place where you enjoy the challenge and the reward of your accomplishments will add another layer to the complexity of your character.

But going back to work isn't just about you or your family. Moms, we *all* need you. Our economy will be stronger with you in it. The *Wall Street Journal* made that point when it analyzed data from the Congressional Budget Office and found that the United States would lose its competitive edge in the future if the overall workforce continues to shrink.[9] When I work on my hiring segments, I always find plenty of jobs in science, technology, engineering, and math, commonly referred to as STEM jobs. But I would love to see more women in these fields because that's where the growth and the money will be. The country is getting older. With baby boomers hitting retirement age, who is going to keep the United States in its current position as the world's largest economy?

Your presence will make a difference. A report by Goldman Sachs Group that focused on Japan's economy discovered that if Japanese women's employment levels rise to 80 percent, the same as that of

9. Lauren Weber, "How to Get More Women into the Workforce," *Wall Street Journal*, http://www.wsj.com/articles/how-to-get-more-women-into-the-workforce-1443600975? cb=logged0.7026360139716417.

Japanese men, the workforce would expand by 7 million people and the economy would grow by 13 percent.[10] Similarly, a McKinsey & Company report found that global growth would expand by $12 trillion dollars by 2025 if women's employment around the world was on par with that of men.[11] The International Monetary Fund estimated economic growth in the United States of 5 percent if women were equal players in corporate culture and the U.S. labor market. In dollars, that would be $4.3 trillion in economic growth.[12] So the numbers make it clear—working women are not just good for the U.S. economy and economies around the world, they're good for families and businesses, too, because the better a nation does overall, the better everyone does.

Another reason for moms to add their presence to the workforce? Because the only way to make the comeback easier for the hundreds of thousands of mothers who want or need to work is for more mothers to make the comeback themselves. Moms can change the system, but they have to do it from within. Take your place at the table and make your voice heard. Agitate from within. Women are 50 percent of the population. We make the majority of the household buying decisions. It is in every company's best interest to listen to mothers

---

10. Yoshiaki Nohara, "Goldman's Matsui Turns Abe to Womenomics for Japan Growth," Bloomberg Business, http://www.bloomberg.com/news/articles/2014-01-21/goldman-s -matsui-turns-abe-to-womenomics-for-japan-growth.

11. Johnathan Woetzel et al., "How Advancing Women's Equality Can Add $12 Trillion to Global Growth," McKinsey & Company, http://www.mckinsey.com/insights/growth /how_advancing_womens_equality_can_add_12_trillion_to_global_growth.

12. Katrin Elborgh-Woytek et al., "Women, Work and the Economy: Macroeconomic Gains from Gender Equity," International Monetary Fund, https://www.imf.org/exter nal/pubs/ft/sdn/2013/sdn1310.pdf.

and take advantage of their collective clout, skills, wisdom, and insight. Remember that every time you go for an interview.

You can do this. Will it be easy? Maybe not. But it's not like this is your first foray into the working world. You got a job once; you can do it again. Besides, when you left the workforce you only turned in your company ID badge, not your brain. If anything, you've got more to offer now than you did before. You just need to prepare and package yourself in a way that proves it. That's where I and the hundreds of women interviewed for this book come in. I promise you, you're not alone. We're here to help you become as much of a success out in the workplace as you have been at home. So let's get started—your comeback is waiting.

2

Plan Ahead.
Way, Way Ahead

I f you're a mom who last put on a suit when *Sex in the City*'s Miranda Hobbes was a working mom's fashion icon, keep reading. You haven't missed the boat. But here's the thing: The advice I'm about to offer is not just for every working woman who thinks she'll want to stay at home with her children one day. It's for every working woman, period. Yes, it will behoove the younger generation to absorb this information early and start implementing it with the idea that one day it will pay off should they decide to have children, take a leave, and make a comeback. But I assure you, almost all of the information in this chapter is applicable to any woman who has already left the workforce and wants to come back. You know why? Because there's little difference between how a woman planning a possible exit should operate and how she'll need to operate once she gets back in.

Quite simply, women are held to a different standard than men in the workplace. We can't be too nice lest we come across as pushovers, but we can't be too assertive lest we be accused of being difficult. We are more frequently interrupted in meetings and have to fight harder to make our ideas heard. We have to prove ourselves in ways that our male counterparts just don't. And if you're a mom—any mom—the bias you face can be even greater. There's actually a term for it: the motherhood penalty. There are many fair and family-friendly employers and companies out there, yet there are still a lot who might assume (maybe even subconsciously, because that's often how bias works) that because you have children, you will be less committed, productive, and effective than someone who does not. Follow these rules, and you'll prove them wrong, whether you're still working and planning an exit or just starting your comeback. This is solid career advice, not just working mom advice.

Rule #1: Work Like You're Never Leaving

If you approach your job as a stopgap, keeping you busy until the day you can leave for your real job—motherhood—it's going to show, and people are going to treat you accordingly. They won't take you seriously because they'll know you're not in it for the long haul, and you aren't invested in the work or the company in the same way they are. So even if you already know deep in your heart that you want to be a stay-at-home mom someday, act as though you've got your eye on the corner office. Not just because it is only right to give your co-workers and supervisors your best, but also because you just never know. It could take you a while to get pregnant. You could discover that you like your job more than you thought you would. There are many reasons why you should want to make yourself indispensable. So be a star. Apply for the promotions. Be a leader and a team player. Go the extra mile. Show the world (and yourself) what you're made of. Be a great professional role model to all the younger, more junior-level women coming up in the ranks.

In addition, be someone people want to work with—punctual,

professional, and personable. Some career experts advise women to keep their work and personal life strictly separate. I don't always agree. Relationships are currency. That doesn't mean you want to be overly emotional (yet another double standard—a man can melt down in a meeting and everyone will admire him for his "passion," while a woman doing the same thing will get accused of being irrational and maybe worse) or bring your personal drama into the office, but do make friends. Make sure to show an interest in other people, their lives and families. Do small favors. Let people know you're on their side and that you care.

Everyone needs allies. The relationships you form now will determine whether your friends cover for you when morning sickness causes you to bolt from your desk to vomit up your breakfast, or help you keep the doors open should you ever want to return after taking a break to stay home with your children. You reap what you sow; the tone you set now will have a direct impact on how your future pregnancy will be received at work. Should you choose not to have children, the 110 percent you put in now will ensure your stellar credibility, status, and reputation.

And don't just focus your attention on your supervisors and managers. Everyone below you on the food chain matters, too. You never know when that twenty-eight-year-old whiz kid from Yale will surpass you on the org-chart and be the one you're answering to upon your return. Those ambitious young people coming up in the ranks—the ones you mentored, helped along, and kept in line— could be your best resources one day. You might have hired them, but while you take a break, they'll be taking a promotion. If you're out for five years with your children, the chances are good they could be the VPs you'll be hitting up for a job by the time you return. They could be the people who will be able to open doors for you. We joke about it in my business all the time: be nice to the good interns—they'll be your bosses one day.

Remember: you will need favors or connections when you're ready to return, whether it's in twelve weeks or twelve years. And if you've been out for those twelve years already, go ahead, track those young people down. Don't be intimidated. They still remember you as the top dog. Carol Fishman Cohen of iRelaunch, a career reentry resource she founded after making her own comeback following a long break from full-time work, calls it the Frozen-in-Time concept—younger people remember you as a kick-ass, take-no-prisoners career woman; their image of you, from the day you left before you had children, is preserved in their minds. They don't know you as the drowning-in-diapers mom, or the one who lacks confidence. Their memory of you is from when you were at the top of your professional game. And there's no reason to let them know any different.

Rule #2: Know Your Company's Maternity Leave Policy

The generosity or lack thereof in your company's attitude toward mothers will stem straight from the top. Rachel Zoe saw that a large chunk of her staff was at the age at which children were going to happen. What did she do? She opened a nursery at work so her mom-staff would stay. Facebook's CEO, Mark Zuckerberg, announced he would take two months of the four months of paternity leave the company makes available to all new fathers. Marissa Mayer, CEO of

Yahoo!, established a sixteen-week leave for new mothers after taking the job in 2012, though by taking only two weeks herself upon
the birth of her son and, more recently, "limited time away" after the
birth of her twin daughters, she didn't set a very good precedent for
the other working moms at the company who might have been planning on taking advantage of the full leave.

Maternity leave policies and the company culture behind them
are the kinds of things that ideally you would want to find out ahead
of time if you can. Maternity leave is not the first thing you want to
ask about during a job interview, but if you can figure it out by asking around or using any resources the company offers, do so. Is there
a nursery on-site? A lactation room? Is there a child-care stipend?
Flextime options? What time do people generally leave the office?
How often do they work on weekends? Look for the signs of a family-
friendly, and especially a mom-friendly, workplace.

But in all likelihood, if you're currently employed you didn't
think to look at the section of the company handbook that explains
maternity leave policies when you accepted your job. Well, now's
the time. Most companies have online resources to help you plan for
your time away from work. And they should also have a company
policy manual outlining their benefits and coverage. Some companies will give you a few weeks off at full pay and then a few additional weeks at reduced pay; some won't pay you at all for any time
you take.

The 1993 Family and Medical Leave Act (FMLA) protects mothers' jobs and preserves their group health insurance while allowing
them to take several weeks of *unpaid* leave to stay home with their
infants, but many companies are exempt, and eligibility depends on

several factors, including the length of time you've been with your employer.[13] If the FMLA doesn't apply, many states have their own maternity leave laws in place. It's worth doing your own research on what your state requires of your company. The National Partnership for Women & Families is a great place to start your research.

It's in your best interest to know your company's policy before you announce your pregnancy at work. One woman interviewed for this book took her maternity leave twenty-five years ago, returning initially part time, then full time years later. When she initially told her boss she was taking her maternity leave, she was floored when he said, "Lucky you. I'd sure love to go put my feet up for a few months, too." She shrugged it off as a sign of the times. Fortunately, she knew her rights and wasn't discouraged by the idiocy of his words.

She returned to work part time while her children were young, and then full time much later. She enjoyed a long and successful career at that company. She enjoyed, too, seeing the overt disrespect she had faced fade away as each new generation of employees brought profoundly different attitudes and perspectives regarding working mothers.

Maybe you're coming back to the workforce and don't think this advice about the company handbook and leave options really applies to you. You're done having kids. I'd strongly suggest being aware of company policy anyway, and whether your company is covered by the FMLA. You might eventually be responsible for aging or ill parents one day and want to know that your job is safe if you need to take time off to care for them. If you, your spouse, or your child gets sick,

---

13. "Wage and Hour Division," U.S. Department of Labor, http://www.dol.gov/whd/fmla/.

it will be good to know what options your company offers. The FMLA doesn't just protect mothers with newborns; among other things, it protects any eligible caregiver who needs to take time off from work to care for an ailing family member.[14]

Women are the primary caretakers in our world, and for mothers that job doesn't stop once their children are more self-sufficient or even grown. Since you can't predict the future, be prepared. Always.

Should you work for a company that is not covered by the FMLA, or you're not eligible, here's where my advice about working as though you're never leaving is doubly important. When you've proved yourself reliable and committed, and have worked on building a good relationship with your boss and colleagues, you'll more likely be met with compassion and understanding should you request more time off, a flexible work schedule, or some other arrangement that allows you to care for your family while holding on to your career.

Rule #3: Build a United Home Front

When you plan a trip, do you hook up the travel trailer and drive off with no supplies and no idea where you want to go, or head to the airport and only decide your destination in front of the departure board? Of course not. Bringing a child into the world is the ultimate adventure, and there will be some things for which you just can't plan. But there are some things for which you absolutely can and

---

14. "Wage and Hour Division," U.S. Department of Labor, http://www.dol.gov/whd/fmla/.

should plan for—just like when you take a trip. You can't assume that any plans you make now won't need some adjustments later on, but the very act of sitting down and trying to think ahead will put you in a better position when you really do have to make decisions than if you just try to wing it as you go.

Money is often the number one thing couples fight about, but you can minimize any risk of conflict or disagreement if you do a financial plan even before you think you need one, and certainly before you have a baby, when fatigue and busyness can cause you to choose convenience and ease over frugality. That's not always a bad choice, mind you. It's just a more expensive one, and one you might feel less pressured to make if you and your partner have thought things through ahead of time.

So schedule a meeting with your partner, pull out paper and a pencil or open up an Excel spreadsheet, and do the math. Apps such as Mint, LearnVest, and BillGuard are good if you prefer everything on your smartphone. A website like Bankrate Inc. is good for mortgage calculations and loans, and Yahoo! Finance is a good overall place for investing news and commentary. MSN Money and of course the Fox Business Network website are other favorites. What does your financial picture look like with another mouth to feed? Outline your spending habits and start making adjustments now so that it's less painful later.

Talk about your jobs. Who will have more flexibility and be able to take days off when the child gets sick or school is canceled or lets out early due to inclement weather? Who has the better leave policy and better medical plan? Who travels more for work, and how realistic is it that either of you will be able to curtail that schedule? How much would one spouse have to earn to comfortably afford for the other to take a few years off to be home while the children are young? Is part-time work an option? How hard could your potential earnings be hit if you take a break, and how will that affect your savings for things like college and retirement? Recognize that if you leave, your company will no longer be making payments into your 401(k), which means any interest you might earn will be based solely on whatever money you have in there now. Assuming a rate of 5 percent, how will that look in forty years?

Any financial planner will tell you it's imperative that your family maintains an emergency money fund. In case of a sudden job loss in the family or another type of emergency like illness or death, you will need enough money to cover six months of the following:

- Rent or mortgage

- Food

- Car payments

- Utilities

- Insurance (car, home)

- Children's expenses, like school tuition, clothing, and extra-curricular classes

- Health insurance

If you don't have this kind of savings on hand now, you'll want to set up a plan for this immediately.

Talk about your careers. Can you afford the loss of job growth that may happen if you decide to stay at home for a period of time with the kids? Will you lose your competitive edge by leaving? Do you care? Will you resent it if other people get promoted over you?

Don't wait until your baby is born and you're in happyland and incapable of seeing the challenges you might face—or worse, until you're back at work and exhausted, stressed, and sniping at your spouse because he hasn't yet figured out where you need him to step up more. You're going to have to be patient with each other no matter what—going from a couple to a trio takes some adjustment. But talking about who's going to do what and when and how as much as you can ahead of time will help you avoid fights later.

Rule #4: Make Sure You Know Your Financial Situation

In addition to making sure you are building savings, make sure you yourself, not just your partner, know what's going on with your finances. The financial planners I spoke to said that the majority of women, even professional and highly educated ones, physically write and mail the actual checks to pay the family's bills, but don't have any additional knowledge about the household's overall financial picture. Zero. They have no idea how much is coming in or going out. They don't know what their mortgage rate is or how much is being invested for retirement. That's a problem in general, but if divorce hits, or worse, death, a mom needs to have a solid understanding of the financial landscape in the home, so she can manage her own finances if she's on her own and working, and so she knows what is available to her in the event of a split. Educate yourself. Know what's happening with the money in your household.

I learned this lesson by watching my great-aunt Rosa Crooks and it's one I will never forget. When my great-uncle Weldon passed away in his seventies, Rosa was still healthy and active. But Aunt Rosa had never written a check, didn't know how to handle the checking and savings accounts, and had no idea what she or Weldon had put away in their savings. In her late sixties Aunt Rosa had to learn everything about money for the very first time. She lived well into her nineties, spending over two decades on her own. I never wanted to be in Rosa's position, and neither should you.

If you are married, and especially if you are married and at home raising kids, you need to maintain a *separate* account with one month's worth of the family's cash set aside *in addition* to the family's holdings. Call it your slush fund, whatever, but have one. Multiple women I interviewed were out of their careers for so long, they actually had no money of their own to use to pay for retraining or to take classes to update their skills. Not a penny. You don't need to keep this account a secret from your spouse, but you should make sure you have something independently held. In fact, both spouses should consider having their own separate bank accounts and operating budgets. All money does not need to be merged.

Keeping your own account has nothing to do with whether you trust your spouse. It has everything to do with financial hygiene that recognizes the high rate of divorce. Should you be forced to return to the workplace because of an acrimonious separation from your spouse, you want to be sure you have the resources to fund the expenses of a job search—clothing, printing, networking, and retraining.

Congratulations, You're Pregnant. Now What?

If you haven't studied your company's maternity policy and discussed a plan with your partner if you have one, get going. Sit down and start doing some financial calculations and talking about how you'd like the next few years to look. Now compare those plans and calculations to your company's maternity policy and make any necessary adjustments. Once your plan is set, you can think about the timing of announcing your pregnancy to your company.

Timing Your Announcement

Take note of how other women in your industry have fared after announcing pregnancies. Are there a lot of working mothers in your business? How about at the top levels? Many women choose to wait until the three-month mark to announce their pregnancies to anyone, but in my field I've known some to wait as long as possible, even until they were showing before breathing a word about it at work. There's always a fear in any newsroom that assignments will shift or opportunities will diminish with a pregnancy announcement. Only you know the biases and double standards of your industry. Don't ever assume they won't be used against you. Think about the women and colleagues you've known who have announced pregnancies in your workplace and ask yourself:

- How were they treated?

- Did you overhear complaints or concerns from them during the course of their pregnancy?

- Did their upward movement at the company seem fair upon their return?

Let this information guide you as you decide when to make your announcement.

Make an Appointment with HR

Whenever you do decide to make your pregnancy public, I recommend your first stop be the human resources department, not your boss's office. This is up to you, but that's my recommendation after speaking to women who've been through the process at the corporate level. There are a lot of issues that need to be factored in before you go on maternity leave, and the human resources person will give you all the guidance and potential protection you might need.

Ideally you will already know the answers to many of the following questions, but ask anyway. You'll want to get specific information on health-care coverage. What are your hospital options, and what payments are covered for doctor visits and infant care? Will you be entitled to your full wages, or will you only get paid a percentage of your current salary? Will the company contribute to your 401(k) while you are out? What about your bonus accrual and vacation days? I recently spoke with someone who when she got pregnant had no idea that her company was going to pay her only a portion of her salary while she was out on maternity leave. You might be stuck with what you find out, since you're already pregnant, but you'll at least want to make sure there is no miscommunication so that nothing comes as a surprise later.

Ask about extended leave. One of my first jobs in television was to fill in for someone who was taking six months' maternity leave. Investigate whether extended leave beyond the twelve weeks offered at your company is an option, and whether you can afford to take it. If you would like to ask for extended leave even if the company doesn't formally offer it, make sure to have a plan written out and be able to make a strong case as to why it will work.

Talk to Your Boss

Now that you've laid the groundwork, done your homework, and decided how long you can or want to stay out, make an appointment to speak with your boss immediately after you see your HR representative. Even if you've got a great working relationship, try to keep this particular conversation professional and to the point. No matter how happy your boss may be for you, these questions are likely what's going through his or her head as you offer up the news:

- How am I going to replace her?

- When is she leaving?

- When is she coming back?

- How will this impact the company?

- How many more times is she going to do this, and how soon?

It's your boss's job and fiduciary responsibility to keep the trains moving with or without you. He or she needs to consider the team. Someone is going to have to cover for you while you're gone. If it's not possible to bring in a temporary replacement, it's possible your team, including your boss, may wind up with extra work on top of their already heavy loads. They may be more than willing—after all, they never know when they'll be the ones who need you to cover for them—but don't underestimate the effect your departure could have on their lives.

More and more bosses are realizing the value of moms and making efforts to make it easy for women to return to work after having children, but the sad reality is that women in their childbearing years often still get treated differently from men of the same age. Manage your boss's expectations by being clear, confident, and unapologetic. Lay out your plan for what the next few months are going to look like and do everything you can to reassure him or her that you've got everything under control.

Set a Return Date

Leave could play out a number of ways. You might think you're coming back, but something comes up weeks into your leave, like a health issue or crisis, that forces you to stay home. Be honest and transparent if that happens. But, if you know you're never coming back, say so right away. *Don't take the leave. Don't take the payments.* It could cost you payback money later—you might end up owing the company salary and health-care costs that you accepted during your leave. Also, think about what a fake-out move like that would do to your professional reputation. If your boss and your colleagues are expecting you to come back, and you don't show up after the allotted twelve weeks, there are going to be some hard feelings. You will have just pulled a major bait and switch. If you need references, you won't get any from this job. Are you ready for that? Why damage your professional reputation when you may want to return to the workforce down the line? Remember the most surprising thing I found as I researched this book: the majority of women I interviewed who planned to never return to work did. Never burn a bridge. Keep your reputation in stellar order.

There are two schools of thought on planning a return date: lock it in and don't. Employment lawyers I interviewed advised that you should always be clear about your intentions, and if you do want to return right away, lock in a start date so there's no ambiguity. Of course, babies often keep their own schedules. Most women I spoke with waited until the very last minute to start their maternity leaves to maximize the number of days they were home with their infants. But you could go into labor two weeks or even two months early. Your baby might be perfectly happy where it is and you could wind up needing to be induced, or deliver by C-section, a few days after your baby's official due date. All of these factors will affect your return. You can't predict any of those things, but, if your company will allow it, wait as long as you can to set the return date.

If you want to negotiate for more than twelve weeks, an open return date, or an alternate work schedule following your return, you will have to know your rights cold. And while you're guaranteed to get your job back, it's not a perfect world. You might be assigned to a different account, a different department, or a client you are less than thrilled about working with. You might be discriminated against (although they would never say it out loud) if they think it's the first of many children to come, and your upward mobility might be capped.

If You Change Your Mind

Planning ahead is the number one thing you can do to make your pregnancy, leave, and comeback go the way you want it to. But as we've discussed, there are plenty of factors that you just won't be able to predict, including this one: no woman ever knows how she is going to feel after having her baby. You can be absolutely certain that you want to stay home, and after three months of changing diapers realize that you'll go crazy if you can't work at least part time. On the other hand, the most hard-charging career women have been known to resign after a week at home with their infants. Now just because your feelings change doesn't necessarily mean your plans can—financial and logistical realities will determine that. But let's say you did genuinely plan to return exactly twelve weeks after you took your leave, and now you just can't bring yourself to leave your child. What's more, you can afford to take a little more time off. Reading the fine print in that company manual will help you know your options.

Stacey was 100 percent certain she would return the second her maternity leave was over, until she wasn't. She was a driven and successful journalist. Two huge life-changing events happened for her at the exact same time: she got pregnant with her first child and was simultaneously offered the position she'd worked toward her entire news career—anchoring a live online newscast. Not only would the job require long hours, it would require a move to New York from California. Despite the challenges, her mind was made up: she would take six weeks and then she and her family were hitting the Big Apple. As her due date approached, she insisted to her managers, her producers, and everyone involved that she was staying the course. She was excited about the baby, but also for the opportunity.

She remembers everyone looking at her with glazed eyes—a look that she later realized meant, "Only six weeks? You're crazy!" They were of course dead-on, because after a couple of weeks at home with her newborn, Stacey extended her stay for her full twelve weeks. Then, frantic to not leave the new love of her life, she grabbed the paperwork she'd signed before departing to see what her options were if she wanted to hold on to that coveted job. Buried in a section of the contract that she hadn't previously read, she found a clause that stated she could negotiate with her manager to work part time postmaternity leave, and that by doing so she would protect her job with the company. She then negotiated a six-month leave of absence, followed by a part-time three-day-a-week gig. She worked that schedule through the birth of her second child.

Stacey's advice: you should expect to change your mind, so read your employee manual thoroughly so you know your options. That clause she didn't read the first time around? It was in a section of the contract titled "If You Choose Not to Return to Work." Stacey hadn't read it because it never occurred to her she wouldn't return to work. So make sure you read everything, whether you think it applies to you or not.

Make a To-Do List

You really can't start planning ahead too early for your comeback, but at the very least I would urge any pregnant employee to create the following to-do list and make sure that everything on it is crossed off before taking maternity leave:

- Check on your credentials. Do you need to maintain a license or credentials to continue practicing in your field? What are the consequences of letting it expire? Also keep in mind that rules do change, so once you're on leave, make a point of doing an annual or twice-yearly check-in with your association or governing body to see if the requirements will remain the same while you're gone.

- Join professional networking groups and maintain the dues and contacts while you're out. Even if networking was never your thing or you had no need for it before, you need it now. You will need it the entire time you're not working, whether you're just taking a brief leave or staying home for several years. These connections will be key to minimizing the pain if you ever try to ease your way back into the workforce. (We'll talk about credentials and networking at length in the next chapter.)

- Update your résumé. Secure letters of recommendation or testimonials from some of the most prestigious colleagues, supervisors, clients, and customers you've worked with in your field. The people you're leaving behind might be MIA by the time you come back to work. Make sure you're armed with the praise you've earned when you exit.

• Create a professional setting at home. Give yourself a space that is yours and yours alone, a place where you can keep a computer, work quietly, and gather your thoughts away from the hustle and bustle of the house. You could convert the guest bedroom to a home office but just a little nook somewhere will be fine. Organizing a small home-office area will make it more likely that you will spend ten minutes every day keeping up with your connections and your industry news. If you have to pull out the computer every time you need to send an e-mail or read the news, you're less likely to do it. And it will be really, really important that you do it. You will need to make that ten-minute professional check-in as routine as brushing your teeth.

Before You Leave ...

You've given your notice, your colleagues threw you a lovely shower in the break room, and your feet are so swollen at the end of the day they're practically spilling out of your shoes. You've tied up as many loose ends as you could and filled everyone in on all your outstanding projects, leaving them with any information they might need. Even if you think you're coming back in twelve weeks, don't leave without taking a few things with you:

- Everyone's online connections: LinkedIn, Facebook, Instagram. Whatever the social network your boss, clients, and colleagues use, don't leave without knowing their handles.

- Personal contact information for bosses and colleagues, including home address, home e-mail, and mobile phone number if you feel the relationship is friendly enough to seek it out. You will want to send out your birth announcement to a home address. Everyone wants to be included in the joy of your life, and taking the time to send such an important piece of real mail will make them feel like a part of your family. Also, having personal contact information—especially an e-mail address—will be crucial if you decide not to return to your job. You never know when you'll need it.

- A list of ongoing projects, initiatives, client contracts, and challenges that the company will be dealing with while you're out. This way, you'll have a reminder of what was going on when you left, and can casually check in via e-mail from home to find out how things are going, offer support or encouragement, and stay a part of the conversation. When one of our executive producers went on maternity leave after having her first baby, I was incredibly impressed that she kept e-mailing me pitches for segments. It kept her on my mind—out of the office, but not forgotten. Her clear interest in what was going on at work made us all excited and eager for her return, and minimized the effects of her absence. In fact, it felt like she never left. This would be a great strategy if you wanted an extended leave. Be there without actually being there. Call it being there-ish.

- A printed copy of your contact list to have at home, even if you're the high-tech-everything-is-digital type. At the very least, back up your contact list on a drive to keep at home. If you have company computers or phones, back up all of that content—especially your personal stuff (though I highly advise against using work phones and computers for personal communications). You never know when that digital information might become unavailable.

- Personal items, effects, and pictures. If for some reason you decide not to return to work, you'll feel better knowing that you don't have to go back into the office to reclaim your stuff, assuming they even let you in the door—many companies are forgoing the standard two-week notice after an employee announces he or she is leaving because of cybersecurity and cyber-theft concerns. You don't want to have to ask someone to gather up all your personal items and send them to you, either. If you do return after your maternity leave, you'll be pleased to find that you have a clean slate and lots of room on your desk to start new projects.

- An ally lined up on the inside before you leave. Stay in touch while you're out so you can keep abreast of who has been coming and going, what projects have been launched, what people are working on, and so forth. You'll want to get this information from someone at the managerial level, too, but you'll probably get more details if you've cultivated a friend on the inside. Some people might disapprove at what could be construed as gossip. I prefer to call it keeping your eye on the action. Call it whatever you like: insider information is valuable, and it will help you upon your return.

No matter how or when or if you're returning to work, leave on a high note. As your mother may have told you, "Never burn a bridge." Be professional and above reproach. You never know how your life will play out and how you will cross paths with old contacts, employers, or employees down the road. You'll probably want to fly out of your office on that final day before maternity leave and not look back, but play it like you're coming back the next day.

Today, you might think you'll never return—but I'll say it a hundred times in this book: most women I interviewed didn't think they'd ever go back to work. But they did. Prepare as though you might. Or maybe you've already left and are trying to come back. If that's the case, once you're back be prepared and flexible all at once. And know this, too: It will work out. You'll make the right decision for your family and your career.

3

Connect, Connect, Connect

My first piece of advice for women who hadn't yet left the workforce was to work as though you were never leaving. My first piece of advice in this chapter is for women who have already left, whether it was ten weeks or ten years ago: start rebranding yourself. Maybe in the years BC—before children—you identified primarily as a working woman, but when the children were born you were happy to identify primarily as a mother. Now that you're going through another change, you need to start seeing yourself a little differently, and you need to get others to see you differently, too. You want to start thinking of yourself as more than "just" a mom. Once you do that, you'll be better able to make the rest of the world see you as more than that, too. And that matters because perception matters. People in general, and employers especially, are often unfairly prejudiced against mothers, especially those who have taken time away from the workforce. They don't tend to think of mothers as the multifaceted, multidisciplined, multitasking powerhouses they really are. Thinking about yourself as a working mom will help you start acting like a working mom. These are the first steps you must take to package yourself to make that projection a reality.

With your new mind-set in place, the next step is demonstrating your new brand to the right people. The more people who know you're looking to go back to work, the greater the chances of your finding the right job and getting the right support. To that end, you'll want to be sure to let friends from past jobs know that you are still a working woman. You'll want to expand your network, introducing yourself to people primarily as a career woman, secondarily as a mom. And you'll want to make sure that you stay connected and maintain your brand by maintaining any credentials you held while working full time.

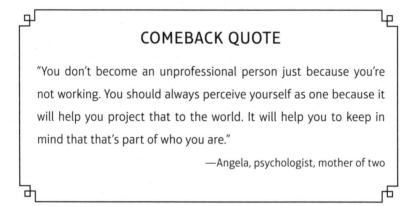

COMEBACK QUOTE

"You don't become an unprofessional person just because you're not working. You should always perceive yourself as one because it will help you project that to the world. It will help you to keep in mind that that's part of who you are."

—Angela, psychologist, mother of two

Stay Connected

Whatever you do, when you leave the workforce, don't let your contacts fade away. Don't check out. The closer in touch you stay with your old workmates, the easier your comeback will be.

If you're reading this and thinking, "Oh no, too late," don't worry about it. Start reengaging, networking, and connecting. Like, right now.

If you're a relatively new stay-at-home mom and one of the many whose main impetus for leaving was that you just didn't want to deal with the stress and complications of trying to work while caring for children, that may not sound very appealing. Walking away from all that was liberating. The whole point of leaving was to allow you to focus your best energy on your family and home life. I know. But take it from other moms who have been there—you do not want to let all your ties to the work world disappear.

When Dania left the workforce to raise her three children, she didn't do much to keep in touch with colleagues and clients and hardly touched her résumé. For eighteen years, she was the epitome of the happy homemaker. She maintained a very tiny embroidery and silk-screen business on the side for fun, but only serviced a small base of existing clients; she didn't do anything to grow the business. Then her husband lost his job. Suddenly, at age fifty-one, with three kids to put through college and an urgent need for income and affordable health insurance, Dania had to go back to work. But finding work in her former industry was no longer an option—with all the technological advancements in her field, she was simply unqualified to go back to anything resembling her old job. She would have to completely rebrand herself to find work.

Dania was a cold case; it would take some serious effort to warm things up. She'd done some volunteer work over the years, but otherwise she was starting from scratch. Her embroidery business was just one small notch above a hobby. Looking back, she wished that as the kids had gotten older she'd tried to stay in touch at least a little bit with the work world so she would have had something to build upon. The process of reconnecting with people in order to establish a network, figuring out what else she was good at and wanted to do, and gaining the credentials and experience that would help her get her foot in the door, took her five full years. Today she would tell anyone stepping out to raise kids to stay connected socially, professionally, and mentally, because you never know when you'll need to tap a resource.

Whether you're just starting out after ten years at home or you gave birth two weeks ago, make it a point to keep one toe in the greater world beyond your family. It doesn't take much time at all, and the payoff can be huge. Here's how:

- Pay attention to the news: During nap time or between school drop-offs, spend at least twenty minutes watching cable news. And if you want to look away from the soccer game for fifteen minutes to scroll through the day's current events, that's OK, too. In the world of instant information, it will keep you sufficiently up to date to be able to participate in the age-old practice of watercooler conversation, which you may want to be able to contribute to again someday. Plus, when you start networking, staying abreast of current events will show people that you are interested in talking about things other than children, and give you a chance to show off your smarts.

- Subscribe to your industry's trade magazines and journals: doctors' appointments and late-night feedings are great times to read about the latest developments in your field.

- Schedule lunch dates: You want to stay in touch with your old colleagues, including those young up-and-comers we talked about in the previous chapter, for two reasons. One, they could be your references one day, and two, they will also help you keep abreast of what's going on in your field. You'll impress any potential employer if you can intelligently discuss and analyze the current events in your industry, especially if they know you've been away from the work world for a while. As you stay in touch with your old colleagues and ask them to fill you in on the latest gossip, take note of how you feel when you're hearing about it. Is it still exciting and interesting to you, or do you increasingly find that you don't care, or that office politics are a turnoff? That will help guide you as you consider where you want to apply for work. Even if you decide to leave your industry altogether, your connections and the information they provide will not be wasted, for you will be able to draw on them during the job application process and during interviews. Don't worry that you can't offer any professional networking advantage to your former colleagues. First of all, you will have been reading up on your industry news. No one can read everything, so you may be able to fill them in on something they didn't already know. Second, if you did a good job of building those relationships while you were still on the job, these are your friends. They will enjoy hearing about your new life. I *love* seeing pictures of my former co-workers' kids. And you know what? These contacts give me a safe place to vent about the working world when I'm frustrated. You can be that safe haven for your ex-colleagues, too. And who knows, they may one day need your advice if they decide they're ready to make a big life change. It's a win-win relationship for both of you.

- Set up a news alert on your e-mail: I subscribe to news alerts with my Yahoo! account. I follow Fox Business and Fox News so that I don't miss anything about my company. You can set up keywords like *pharmaceuticals*, *sales*, or *nursing*, then add a second keyword to get specific posts about your specialty such as *software* sales or *pediatric* nursing. When the *Wall Street Journal* writes about your former business and job category, the article will be sent right to you.

- Be the consumer: if it's applicable, accept the role of consumer in your former business (medicine, retail, and grocery are the easiest). A woman I spoke to who once worked in sales before leaving to stay at home signed up to be a mystery shopper when her kids were young. She loved the extra income, and she was able to monitor the salespeople as a consumer. During nap time, she'd write up her reports. Most companies subscribe to services like this, so why not make the most of that trip to Macy's or Walmart?

Form New Connections

Once you've rebranded yourself as a working woman and are up to date with your existing network, your next step is to, well, get networking to increase your connections. The word *networking* probably makes you think, OMG, now I need to join multiple organizations, and go to expensive and time-consuming lunch- and cocktail-hour events. I need to get cards made and printed. What will I wear?

Not so. Networking just means asking around and starting conversations. With anyone, anywhere.

What's more, it's indispensable. It will help you do all of the following:

- Give you a chance to meet new contacts

- Expand your field of connections

- Help you get the word out about who you are and what you do

- Allow you to connect with industry insiders

- Keep you informed about your old industry or sector, or about a new one that might interest you more

Diligent and determined, Dania spoke to everyone she could find, and would strike up conversations just about anywhere. One day, with some background research and the exploitation of both her small cottage-industry business and some luck, she found a resource in the strangest place: her daughter's soccer field. She had seen a posting for a sales job at a chemical company that intrigued her. She had sold her embroidery work. She knew it was on a small scale, but she hoped the skills would translate. She knew she was a little bit out of her element and that she was going to be intimidated if she actually got the job, but she wasn't in a position to be picky. Plus, she realized that the father of one of her daughter's teammates had a high position at the company she was eyeing. Wondering if he could help her, she began talking to him at their daughters' soccer games. She made sure to let him know that she had managed the team for years, so he knew her organizational skills were exemplary. After a few conversations, he seemed impressed by her and referred her for the job. She got it. Going back to the work world was like going to a foreign country, and struggling to follow the lingo of this field that was altogether new to her felt like learning a foreign language. But she figured it out, and within a few months she felt comfortable and competent in her entry-level position. She spent one very successful year at the company. It may not have been her dream job, but it did exactly what she needed it to do: fill some deep holes on her résumé. That experience, which she landed through networking, coupled with her entrepreneurial skills from years of running a business, helped her land a new gig.

Networking has certainly been the key to my success at every level of my career. When I was a flight attendant in my twenties, I had college friends who worked in broadcasting jobs in Phoenix, and when one of them moved to San Francisco, she helped me land my first internship at the CBS station there. (I had moved to San Francisco for a new adventure, only to realize that I was ready to use my degree in communications to pursue a television career.) That internship led to one job, then another, and finally to my position at KRON TV.

I thought that once I arrived in New York at MSNBC I would work at that one network for at least a few years. I'd succeeded in one of my goals and landed a network job! Check! I thought that though I would continue to connect with people, I wouldn't need to keep networking with the same level of enthusiasm I once had. Well, not so fast. As it turned out, that networking would open up a door at Fox News—a move that eventually gave me an opportunity to become part of the team that launched the Fox Business Network.

When I first came to New York I knew a total of three people, so I had to start all over again building my professional and personal network. It never occurred to me, though, that the two might intertwine. When I left MSNBC after just one year because I wasn't "the right fit" for the job, I was devastated and spent the next two months questioning whether or not I had the thick skin to stay in television news at the cable network level. It wasn't until I saw Janice Huff of WNBC doing a live shot at the Macy's Thanksgiving Day Parade that I realized I missed television news. So I picked myself up "by the bootstraps," as my grandad used to say, and started to make a few phone calls to people I'd met during my first year in New York.

Luckily, a friend of mine who worked at another network suggested I reach out to a producer she knew at Fox News Channel, which eventually led to my interview with Mr. Roger Ailes himself. They were launching the Fox Business Network and were looking for business journalists. This changed my life completely, personally and professionally.

My point: you never, never know what an e-mail, or two or three, or a connection, or two or three, can lead to. If you want to make a comeback—even if it's years away—you have to explore every possible person, event, job posting, and industry lead you come across.

COMEBACK QUOTE

"Network. Network. There's one specific network piece that I see out in the suburbs: moms who socialize in a coed fashion and some who really end up on the women's side of the party, the women's side of the table or the barbecue or whatever. And it's really important to keep up relationships with the men and the women because these could be connections, or they're someone who knows somebody. The more connected you are to people, the more likely they are to remember you or recommend you when some opportunity comes up. That means men, too."

—Kylie, librarian, mother of three

Don't Be Your Own Worst Enemy

Almost every mother I spoke with for this book, whether she came back as a CEO, lead manager, sales associate, or counter girl, admitted that feelings of insecurity had slowed down her job hunt or kept her from applying for certain positions or reaching out to people. They felt insecure because they'd been out of the game, because they were returning as working moms instead of working women, and even because of their age. They worried people would reject them, judge them, and not take them seriously. My advice: Don't listen to that little voice in your head poisoning you with all the reasons why you can't do it. I'm telling you, you can. Everyone, even the most successful individuals, feels insecure sometimes. The trick is to ignore that voice and not to let your insecurities get in your way. Let them go, or they could derail your career success. You are smart. You have skills. Believe in yourself.

The "return-to-work experts" at iRelaunch suggest the following tips for building your confidence while developing your networks:

- First, get back up to speed in your field, or if you're changing fields, learn as much about the new one as you can, because your confidence is going to come from your knowledge and your ability to converse and interact with people in your chosen field. If you don't know yet where you're going to wind up, stay on top of things in the field you left. It might not be where you end up, but it will be a great place to start when you do plan your return.

- Practice talking out loud about your background and your interest in returning to work. It's not enough to say the words in your head—you need to say them out loud. Speak with nonjudgmental friends and family first, then start telling others. The idea is that the more you practice talking about your background and your interest in returning to work, the better you'll sound, and the better you sound, the more confident you'll feel.[15]

I know this works. When I was still employed as a Southwest Airlines flight attendant, I had begun thinking about pursuing what I'd studied in school: communications and broadcasting. I started talking to the pilots, flight attendants, and in some cases the passengers about my

---

15. Interview with Carol Fishman Cohen, iRelaunch.

future television career. I also started talking to friends in Phoenix, including my friend who was a producer at a local Phoenix television station. She ended up helping me secure that San Francisco television station internship after we both moved to the Bay Area. You never know where things can lead. Saying something out loud was a huge part of my transition from the airline industry to broadcasting. I called myself a journalist long before a paycheck confirmed it to be true.

Know Your Story

Why did you leave the workforce? What did you do before becoming a mom? Why do you want to come back now? People are going to ask, and you need to come up with an answer that isn't "I never wanted to be anything but a mother," and "We couldn't afford for me to stay home anymore." It may be true, but neither one is going to compel an employer to risk taking a chance on you, and they may discourage contacts from sticking their necks out on your behalf as well.

Here's a list of questions to ask to help generate your story line. Write your answers down and rewrite them a hundred times. Run them by a relative to make sure they make sense. Everybody needs a good editor.

- How did you land your first job out of college?

- What was your thought process when you first decided to take time off from work?

- If you're continuing an existing career—what did you most love about it? What was its allure?

- If you're changing gears, what's drawn you to the new challenge? Why are you excited about it?

Come up with a positive elevator pitch that explains who you are and what you'd like to accomplish as you reenter the workforce. For example, instead of saying you want the job because "your family needs the money" you could say "I've loved my recent time at home, but I miss the challenge and adrenaline rush of the corporate world." Keep it simple and be direct when asked a question. Try to share your story as often as possible so it feels natural and comfortable as you tell it. It should be strong and succinct and market you in the best light.

Where to Go

Formal Networking Events

These are useful and can be important for making connections, especially if they're field specific. Most cities have networking groups dedicated to helping entrepreneurs, women, minorities, small businesses, and professionals of all kinds find and support one another. A quick Google search will help you locate them and get their events on your calendar. There's no reason to be shy—everyone will be there for the exact same reason. Plus, an hour away from the dishes and diapers in exchange for a glass of wine and some adult conversation is always fun!

You can also double-dip or multitask by networking in places you're already frequenting like the ones that follow.

Playgrounds and Playgroups

Think about how many other moms you end up chatting with in the course of a week while your kids are playing. They might be stay-at-home moms like you, but they know people. This is a great place to start practicing your story, too, because it should be a comfortable, low-pressure environment for you. People always shine when they feel physically and emotionally safe. Typically, when we are feeling out of place, we try harder, and we end up actually coming across as unlikable.

Pediatrician's Office

Your doctor sees lots of moms and dads, and some will love the opportunity to talk about something that doesn't involve colic, fever, or playground injuries. For example, if you are seeing the pediatrician for a routine visit, and he or she asks, "So how's everything going?" you can casually say, "Well, I've been thinking about going back to work." Chatting with the doctor about your job search is one of the best resources you have at your fingertips.

Local Chamber of Commerce

Sign up for the e-mail list or newsletter from your town or city's Chamber of Commerce. They have lots of events you can attend, and many are community- and kid-friendly. Businesses are members of the Chamber, and you never know who is running the charity bake sale. CEOs are people, too, and many of them volunteer at these types of events.

School

I can't believe how many moms I interviewed who told me they ended up conducting their best networking at their child's school. They made connections through other parents, of course, but teachers, the principal, the office staff, and even the school nurse can all be valuable resources to you. Once you get your story straight and know what you want to do when you go back to work, tell them all about it. Everyone knows someone.

Coffee Shops, the Supermarket, Big-Box Stores, Bookstores, Pet Supply Shops, Pharmacies, Dry Cleaners, Locksmiths, Shoe Repair Shops, Gyms ...

You can network anywhere! Job hunting is a bit like dating: you never know who you're going to meet at Starbucks. If you're chatting with a stranger, sniff around. Ask questions. Track down leads. You just never know who works where and whom they might know.

Networking might feel a little uncomfortable at first, which is all the more reason to do it now. Practice *before* you actually need a job. Keep things casual and fun and only occasionally divert the conversation to discuss work prospects. No one wants to talk shop all the time or feel like they're being used.

CONVERSATION STARTERS

- What does your husband/wife do?
- Where did you work before you had kids?
- I used to work at XYZ (company). Do you have any friends or relatives who still do or who work in that field?
- Do you belong to any professional organizations?
- How did you get your start?

You'll be surprised how willing people are to connect with you, and they love to talk about themselves. I've learned as a reporter that people love to talk about their lives, their careers, their experiences, and in some instances their personal problems. How do you think Barbara Walters gets all those celebrities to cry? She asks questions, then just *listens*.

Calm Your Nerves

If the idea of networking events still makes you nervous, here are some tips that have always worked for me.

- Think about a networking event like it's a reality TV show and you've got thirty minutes to meet ten new people. Have a goal in mind of how many business cards you want to get, or how many connections you want to make. Ten business cards? Five phone numbers? Use that goal to keep you from getting stuck for too long in any single conversation and ensure that you mingle enough. Go! As you bounce from person to person, make fun of the fact you are all at a budget hotel conference room event. Don't take yourself too seriously: "I'm here for the cheddar puffs." Remember that everyone else in attendance is there for the same reason you are. You belong there as much as anyone else. Personalize the experience as though you were hanging at your kids' soccer game (and maybe you are). Have fun and relax! If alcohol is served, go ahead and have one drink, and if you are in a great group and having a great time, then two drinks, but that's it. And of course you don't have to drink. When I don't want to, I order sparkling water or seltzer with some lime. Alcohol may be a social lubricant, but I assure you no one will care or think less of you if you're not drinking.

- Navigating an event with a plate of food can be hard. With cocktail apps, you may find yourself distracted by the act of balancing your glass and your plate when you really should be focusing on your conversation with one of the managers from that company you've had your eye on. And sitting down at a table with a full plate of food can kill your energy to the point where you start thinking about pulling an Irish good-bye. I always eat something light before I arrive at an event, especially if I allow myself to have one glass of wine while I'm there. I may snack or pick at the dinner if one is served, but I want my focus to be on the conversations I'm having, not the dried-out chicken breast. Let's be honest, the food at these functions is never that great anyway!

- Don't start the conversation pitching yourself. Right off the bat, people will be ready to back away. Start with a personal, friendly conversation (see the tips on the cold call on page 64). Every conversation is a first date with every person you meet face-to-face at an event, a game, or a party.

Online Networking

The beauty of online dating is that people can sit at home, in their pajamas, and search for potential mates. The same goes for networking for a job.

But don't actually wear your pajamas. Put on something that could be considered business casual—at least from the waist up—and sit down at your desk, especially if you decide to call people. There are a few reasons for this.

You never know when someone will suddenly say, "Hey, long time no see! Let's Skype." Or suddenly your cell phone rings and you see that the person you've been chatting with on Facebook is now calling you on FaceTime. They know you're there, so there's no ignoring the call. No one will expect to see you in a suit jacket and makeup, but impressions matter, and you always want to present yourself in the most professional, put-together manner possible.

People act more professionally when they're dressed more professionally. If you get on a call, you want to sound focused. And don't forget to take notes while you talk.

At home, from your computer, you can keep up with friends and colleagues in many ways.

E-mail

It's old-fashioned, but it works. In this age of texts and Facebook accounts, the only thing more personal than a handwritten letter these days is an e-mail message. Take the time to write a short note to friends from high school and college, former colleagues and clients. It doesn't have to be a missive, but show interest in their lives and make sure to ask questions about their work. Save their answers so the next time you reach out you can refer back to what they said. "How did you wind up resolving that problem with accounts payable?" "I've been thinking about that client who gave you such a headache. What happened with that?" It shows that you're paying attention and that you are still interested in the professional world.

Facebook

Facebook can be a mom's best networking tool. Make sure to friend former colleagues (better yet, friend them before you leave). If their posts don't regularly show up in your feed, make sure to seek them out and "follow" them, and check the box that says *following* if it's not automatically checked. When they post something, hit the *like* button or, even better, leave a comment.

Make sure that you post regularly, too. You don't have to share too much personal information if you don't want to, and you don't even have to post pictures of your kids if that makes you uncomfortable—many people have strict rules about what they will and won't reveal on the site. But do post a healthy mix of status updates about the innocuous things that happen to you during the day or causes you're involved in so that anyone who is "friends" with you can get a sense of your personality and passions. You should also post articles that show you're still reading and still interested in the world beyond your children. Accompany these articles with a comment that shows you're also thinking about the content and its implications, not just clicking on headlines. Your Facebook friends will be among the first people you'll reach out to when you need to start your job search.

When Gina got pregnant with her first child, she knew that a career chasing breaking news was not conducive to raising children, especially with a husband who worked long hours and traveled often. But as she put it, "Once a news junkie, always a news junkie." She was a stay-at-home mom, but she was a well-informed stay-at-home mom, keeping up with the business, the blogs, the websites—all of it. She did it because it was in her nature, but the by-product was that she always knew what was going on with her former colleagues. Facebook made staying connected with the people she knew in media even easier. She'd signed up as soon as her child was born and she realized she wasn't going back to work. She knew that perhaps one day public relations, with its more stable hours, would be in her future, so keeping a connection to the outside world was critical.

She'd read articles and posts while the baby slept or nursed. She said that even though some people worried that Facebook was a time-suck, she actually felt it was a more efficient way to stay connected than e-mailing busy people all the time to check in. Gina called it keeping tabs. There was a flipside, too: she never faded from her friends' and colleagues' minds because they saw what she was up to every day. Social media gave her a way to have intelligent conversations with people whom otherwise she might rarely get to see.

Eventually, three or four years after she left her job, Gina started a consulting firm of her own, targeting her former colleagues to pitch her clients—hoping she could land a story about them on her former TV network. Those Facebook connections helped make her return almost seamless. She didn't have to study or catch up or reconnect with anyone because she'd never really disappeared. She'd already laid all the groundwork bit by bit. Gina would recommend that every mom, no matter how long they've been at home or plan to stay home, do the same—regardless of how much or how little time they have available to do so. It's a small effort that will pay off big in the end.

Twitter

If you're unfamiliar with Twitter it may take you a few tries to figure out how to tweet and retweet properly and the best way to use a hashtag, but it's not rocket science and there are plenty of books and websites available to help you. But do try to get comfortable with it, because it's an excellent information and networking resource.

Use it to follow the latest posts from your favorite parenting magazine, your friends, your former co-workers, the local newspaper, and companies that you are interested in. Retweet and reply to multiple posts as much as possible so they see that you are engaging with them. Not only does this interaction keep you in the loop, it also helps you build your social media network, a prerequisite for almost every professional today.

The great thing about Twitter is that it allows you to connect with people in your industry or sector that you don't already know. Find people who appear to work in your arena. Follow them, and follow the people they follow.

Another benefit is that everyone can see who *you* follow. Translation: whom you decide to follow says a lot about you on a professional and personal level. Strike up conversations. The rule to using Twitter successfully is to be broad: stick with industry tweets much of the time, but mix things up by tweeting about a sport or a show or something random that widens your field.

Also remember that with Twitter and all social media, timing matters: most people with jobs check in at 6 a.m., 9 a.m., and noon (East and West coasts accounted for). There's nighttime action as well—same hours, but p.m. Be strategic if you're tweeting something and hoping for a response. And you do want a response, because Twitter is all about starting conversations and making connections—which is exactly what networking is all about.

Instagram

Sometimes a picture really is worth a thousand words. It's certainly what makes Instagram so great—especially for women who might be introverted or shy. Without words, without working too hard to be witty, we can use a picture to articulate our thoughts or tap into common bonds in an instant. It's a great way to connect with like-minded people. Instagram is one of the most popular ways to engage with people and have some fun with pictures. You can post images of your kids to your network, but you can also watch and follow former co-workers, friends, and family, and "like" or comment on their posts.

Facebook and Instagram are linked, so you can automatically link to your established Facebook friends to follow them on Instagram. You can also follow people you don't know, further widening your network.

According to a CareerBuilder survey, as of 2014, 43 percent of employers use social media to find out more about potential hires and another 12 percent said they planned to start soon.[16] This is in your favor. Cultivate the best online persona you can, the one that shows them what an interesting and valuable contribution you could make to their company. Share articles with commentary that shows employers you're thinking about issues that concern them. At the very least, it will make them see that you'd be someone they'd like to work with, and maybe ensure that you get a call back.

Keep in mind, too, that social media can be a double-edged sword. Make sure there is nothing in your public social media feeds that you wouldn't want a potential employer to see.

Alumni Groups

It seems to have started with Classmates.com, but now there are a thousand ways to find your old high school, college, and grad school connections. You can probably find alumni groups for your old sorority, sports teams, academic groups, and social clubs. You can join these groups on LinkedIn and Facebook, where they give you the opportunity to see where your old friends and classmates have landed professionally as well as personally. I admit it, my college boyfriend has the

---

16. "Number of Employers Passing on Applicants Due to Social Media Posts Continues to Rise, According to New CareerBuilder Survey," CareerBuilder, http://www.careerbuilder .com/share/aboutus/pressreleasesdetail.aspx?sd=6%2F26%2F2014&id=pr829&ed=12 %2F31%2F2014.

cutest kids, and it's fun to see him on Facebook. He also holds a senior position at a company I cover as a business journalist. It's a win-win.

Keep in mind that you don't have to network for a long time every day. You should discipline yourself to do it once a month or every two months while you're not searching, and then once a week when you kick it into high gear. Of course, more is better. If you can set aside an hour every week or one week out of every month, great. If you've only got ten minutes here and there, try setting up a rotation: Mondays are Facebook, Tuesdays are Twitter, Wednesdays are cold calls . . .

Wait. Cold calls? Cheryl, you want me to make cold calls?

I do.

When you find someone who has information you need, or who you really think can help you, you're going to need to make a direct ask. The trick is to do it without sounding pushy or desperate.

How to Make a Cold Call

I know you're thinking, Easy for you to say, Cheryl. You cold call for a living. That's true. But the reason it's easy for me is not just because it's in a reporter's DNA, it's also because I do it all the time. I promise you the first time I made a cold call I was as nervous as you might be. And then it got easier. It'll get easier for you, too, once you start, especially if you follow these tips to striking up networking-worthy conversations.

- Let's say you want to have a conversation with the person in charge of hiring new accounting recruits at your local tax preparation office. A quick call to the front desk or an online search should give you a place to start with a name, an e-mail address, and/or a phone number. If you are able to get through to that person's direct line, introduce yourself and ask them for a quick moment of their time. My favorite opening line is "I know you are really, really busy." (Most people at desk jobs are not *that* busy, and they love the compliment when you hand it out.) Then if the person seems willing to have a conversation, try to work in topics like weather, location, sports . . . start with anything personal. If you found out in your research about them *when you Googled their name* that they tweeted about the Giants-Cowboys game, make a football reference.

- Don't contact anyone on a Monday morning, when everyone is cranky and setting up his or her week. Call Monday afternoon at the earliest. Tuesday and Wednesday are really good because most people are feeling optimistic about the week and are getting productive. Thursday is almost Friday so be careful. Friday they check out.

- Try to mirror your contact's energy or personality on the phone, because you can tell if someone is distracted or rushed. If they seem up for mild chitchat, you can do the same. If they are quick and curt, kept it tight. Say, "I know you are busy. What's the best way to send you my information, or can I give it to you in person?" Make sure you are valuing their time, and you're also acknowledging that it's a lot to ask them to listen to you for five minutes.

- I don't like it when a public relations person gives me a cold call and jumps into a pitch for a story without saying anything personal, not even a nice hello. Sometimes they pretend they know me when they don't! And I hate those e-mails that remind me about the time we talked, except I know for a fact we didn't. Just be honest, represent what you want in a nice way, be straightforward. Also, try not to be boring. You've got charm and wit. Use them.

• Here's a sample opener: "Hi, my name is Cheryl. I know you are busy, but I wanted to reach out to you to get some information for xxx purpose. I was wondering if you have a couple of minutes to discuss xxx."

You want to make an ask, but you want to make it the right one. Here's the wrong ask:

"Will you hire me?" You might ask that later, but not now. Instead, try:

• "Do you have time for a meeting (or call or coffee)?" Face-to-face meetings have greater impact.

• "Can you review my résumé for me to make sure it meets today's standards?"

• "What's the best way to get a start in your industry?"

• "Is there anyone else you might suggest I contact?"

• "Can I follow up with a call later?"

Keep Your Credentials Up to Date

Just as important as maintaining your connection with people is the maintenance of your professional qualifications. I cannot stress this one enough—don't let your credentials lapse. Set markers in your calendar. Is there an annual review? Is there an application you need to fill out every few years? What about testing and upkeep? Stay on top of it all. The consequences could be severe if you don't.

After giving birth to her first child in 2006, Nancy, a doctor, decided to start working part time. After giving birth to her second and then third child, she left medicine altogether to be a stay-at-home mother. Eight years later, she realized that as the children were growing older they needed her unlimited attention less and less, and that one day she'd want to go back to practicing medicine. She realized if she waited much longer, doing so would be difficult. What she didn't know was that she'd already let too much time lapse. In fact, waiting much longer might have put an end to her chances of ever practicing medicine again.

A few years earlier, she and her family had left the East Coast where she was licensed and moved to California. Normally such a move wouldn't have been a problem, but because so much time had gone by since she had first received her license, the state of California required that she get a new one. It took Nancy a series of interviews, exams, and a yearlong fellowship in Nevada that took her away from her family for an entire year to finally get relicensed and be able to practice medicine in California.

On the upside, Nancy made the most of her experience. Rather than just do the bare minimum required for her license, she took a little extra time to broaden her area of expertise and her credentials, sub-stantially upgrading her skills and placing her in a new pay category.

Kerry, on the other hand, always thought that she would eventually go back to work as a physical therapist when her kids were older, and intentionally set out to make sure she was doing what was needed to keep her credentials up to date. She admits, though, that once she was surrounded by children and managing a household, there were moments when she thought about letting it all lapse.

"I definitely had it in the back of my mind, I better not let it expire, but in my heart I thought, I'm going to raise my kids and then I'm going to be volunteering and then I'm going to be a grandma. I'll never work again. I loved being home and I loved being a mom. But I remem-bered the parting words of our professor during the graduate program: 'Do not let your certification expire because you will never be able to pass that board certification exam again.' I remember at the time pooh-poohing, thinking, How stupid is this? But it is so true. I have friends who were nurses and other allied health professionals who let it expire, and what a nightmare they've had trying to recertify."

To keep current, Kerry had to maintain thirty of what the physical therapy field calls contact hours. Some contact hours could be earned through classes, some of which could be taken online or through live streaming. But many contact hours have to be hands-on to ensure ther-apists are keeping up their manual skills when working with patients coping with or recovering from neurological or physical injuries.

Then Kerry did something interesting. She started teaching anat-omy and physiology for an online college. It forced her to keep her knowledge fresh, plus she could do the work from home and fit it in around the family schedule. She graded papers at night after the chil-dren went to sleep.

When the family made a move to a new city, Kerry took the opportunity to start working with patients again for a few hours a week to keep her hands-on skills sharp. The kids were in school by then, and Kerry and her husband realized that without her bringing in income, it was unlikely they would be able to pay for all three children's college tuitions. Since protecting the kids from accumulating too much college debt was important to them, now seemed like a really good time to start transitioning back to the workplace. Kerry hoped that she would be able to turn her part-time job into a full-time position when she was ready. A couple of years later, that's exactly what she did.

A Few Things to Remember

- Credentials vary from state to state, so if you move, check ahead to learn what your new requirements might be.

- Some of the associations through which you earn credentials can actually help you find a job. In fact, while you're out of the workplace you might consider getting involved in some capacity with the state-licensing group for your industry so that you make contacts that could prove helpful when you're ready to return to work.

- Oversight associations are also great resources for staying up to date and involved in your profession. Sign up for the e-mails and stay informed.

Give Yourself Choices

The mothers I spoke to who enjoyed the smoothest transitions back into the workforce were those who left themselves room for choice. You don't want to be backed into a corner. Those who didn't wait too long, or until their entire professional landscape had changed, and gave themselves plenty of time to prepare for their comeback, had an easier time finding the right job than those who for whatever reason had to suddenly jump in and take what they could get. If at all possible, you've got to lay down some groundwork—and managing your connections is the best way to start doing that. Whether you're knee-deep in planning your return now or unlikely to start for a year or two, rebranding, connecting, networking, and staying professionally relevant are the keys to the stay-at-home mom's comeback.

4

Crafting a Killer LinkedIn Profile and Résumé

I f you've been out of the workforce for a long time, you will likely be startled by how much technology has changed the way we apply for jobs. Moms of a certain age will remember all the stamps and envelopes they once licked as they mailed off sixty copies of their résumé to every potential employer that posted a job opening in the newspaper. I remember the first time I ever created a résumé. I chose special paper and envelopes because I thought it said something about me, my character, if I chose beige or blue stationery.

Today you're most likely going to fill out job applications online and upload a digital copy of your résumé. Good news! The new process is fast and cheap and you can do it while dinner is heating up in the oven. Not-so-good news—you still need a résumé. You'll need a LinkedIn profile, too, which is really just a big public résumé. And I know that for almost every one of you reading who has walked away from her career and then decided to return to work, the idea of putting one together or trying to list your marketable skills after so much time off is terribly daunting. But it doesn't have to be, especially because you're reading this chapter, which contains all the information every mom who stays home needs to highlight and package her accomplishments and skills so that she stands out from the competition.

LinkedIn

Before we talk about résumés, we're going to talk about LinkedIn, which may be the most important job-hunting tool you could use today. That said, I'm slightly embarrassed to admit that I didn't use LinkedIn until I started reporting and writing this book. Granted, the news business works slightly different from corporate America, and since I have the greatest gig on the planet and an agent who handles the business side of things for me, I never really felt the need to polish up my résumé and figure out how LinkedIn works. But that was a mistake, because the same is true for me as it is for you or any other woman: we should always be prepared for anything.

Faced with the need to link myself in so I could better explain the process to you, I sought help from an expert: Katie Fogarty, the creator of LinkedIn Reboot, a personal consulting business. Katie creates powerful, optimized LinkedIn profiles for executives and entrepreneurs, career switchers, moms looking to reenter the workforce, and college and grad students looking to launch their careers. Her specialty is helping people get back into the workforce after a short or extended gap by polishing their LinkedIn profiles. Katie sees LinkedIn as a fantastic career reentry tool for moms for many reasons, and for one big one in particular: "Women are wired to connect and share, which makes social networks such as LinkedIn a natural fit. Used correctly, LinkedIn is an unparalleled networking platform, one that offers moms looking to return to work after off-ramping the chance to present their professional narrative far more powerfully than a paper résumé."

In other words, it allows you to tell your story in a way that a résumé cannot.

According to Katie, LinkedIn allows moms to:

- Be transparent about what they've been up to and why they're getting back to work.

- Reveal their chosen path and highlight what's important to their next career move.

- Present themselves accurately and not hide the fact that they're moms.

Unlike a résumé, LinkedIn doesn't limit you to a one-line job objective and a list of bullet points. Instead, it allows you to create a document that could be applicable for a wealth of different jobs, and the first thing people see below your name is a summary section where you can write a brief but descriptive explanation of not only who you are, but also where you want to go. Done right, it can give possible employers a chance to get a sense of your voice and personality in a way that a résumé just can't. You can put your time away from the workforce in context, and explain how you can still bring value to employers. Then you can use the rest of your profile to build on that story. What's great, too, is that this is a story you can easily update and keep developing as you prepare for your comeback. If you take on a new leadership role within your community, even at the volunteer level (there's a Volunteering Experience section just for this purpose) or acquire a new skill or get new certifications, you can get that information up on your profile immediately and make sure that your settings are such that your connections can all see it when you do. You don't want to be constantly updating, but you do want to look for reasons to get your name and face to appear in other people's feeds. Because if one of your connections sees that you're volunteering for Meals on Wheels, and one of your connections is a big supporter of Meals on Wheels, you might just have an in.

LinkedIn is important. Recruiters use it to find talent, and potential employers will check it to learn more about you, either before or after your interview. I know one PR professional who checks prospective hires' connections before making a commitment. If they aren't connected to the main players in media in his field, how can they pitch stories? But no pressure. Don't be intimidated. While you'll want to make sure that everything is done exactly right, you really should only need a few hours, a weekend at most, to get your LinkedIn profile up and running. This is an exciting moment! You're hanging up your shingle, letting people know you're ready for business. You'll see—you're going to be able to give them lots of reasons to walk through the door.

To begin:

• Fix your privacy settings optimization so you don't broadcast every update you make as you're refining or building your profile. You do this by turning off your activity broadcast. Once you're set, turn it back on.

• Create a custom URL with your name. Mine reads: www .linkedin.com/cherylcasone. If you go to the Help Center, enter Customize Your Public Profile URL into the search-and-question bar and you'll be walked through how to do this.

- Get recommendations from past employers—aim for one from each place you've worked, and not necessarily from your boss. Three recommendations deem a profile complete by LinkedIn.

- Stay connected online just like you do in real life. Use Twitter, Facebook, and the tool that allows you to see who in your e-mail contacts has a LinkedIn profile, too.

- Make your skills section sing. In Katie's words, "Bang your drum!" Skills are keyword searchable and will boost the number of eyeballs that land on your profile. You can add up to fifty. Make the first ten in each category the strongest. This will boost endorsements, too.

- Join groups. According to LinkedIn, your profile is five times more likely to be viewed if you join and remain active in groups. Find professional organizations that match your initiative, or professional women's groups.

- Update your profile quarterly.

- Look to others for inspiration. Check your mentor's page or that of a leader in your industry. What have they done? How have they set up their profile? Learn from them.

- Never leave required sections blank.

- Use specific descriptions to demonstrate successes in whatever you've accomplished in fund-raising or volunteer work.

- Use modern and industry-appropriate language—techies often talk about the "digital space," for example—but don't use empty jargon. Say what you mean.

Katie shared some samples of summaries and rewritten profiles, all designed to hide and fill gaps. All of these were selected from profiles belonging to stay-at-home moms who landed gigs.

- *My work is defined by strong quantitative, analytical, and communications abilities—delivered with an emphasis on customer-focus and cross-functional team building. I measure success as being effective for others.*

- *I love books and believe in the power of libraries. Information is a potent commodity and there is power in sharing it with others.*

- *In my past life, I was a worldwide creative coordinator. When I became a mom fourteen years ago, I said good-bye to the structure of a traditional workplace and hello to serial entrepreneurship and the free agent economy. I went on to launch and later sell a start-up.*

- *Why did I switch paths from finance to library science? I decided it was time to return to my roots, marrying my interest in information and data with my passion for academia and learning new subjects.*

FIVE *MOM-MISTAKES* NOT TO MAKE ON LINKEDIN

1. **Cutesy doesn't cut it.** Don't try to hide a gap in your work years by titling your time at home "CEO of the Smith Household." Everyone knows that being a mom is work, but no employer wants to see you referring to car pool duty as "logistics management."

2. **No dog, no husband, no baby.** Your profile picture should be exactly that—you in professional attire and preferably professionally photographed. Save the adorable vacation snap of you and your little one for Facebook.

3. **Selling yourself short.** Work is work and if you've spent time at home in active volunteer roles, or adding skills through continuing education, that information belongs on your LinkedIn page. Present a 360-degree picture of yourself—an employer in the wellness industry will appreciate your passion for yoga or running, even if they are hiring you for an HR role.

4. **No apologies necessary.** Staying at home with your kids does not need to be defended on LinkedIn—or anywhere. Avoid the temptation to explain your choices and stick to using LinkedIn's valuable real estate to both sell yourself and let employers know how you will deliver on their needs.

5. **Saying nothing.** Not apologizing is not the same thing as not explaining. Employers are busy—they don't have time to decode your work history. If you've taken time off from work say so directly, but don't make it a focus. Build your profile so that it clearly conveys your value proposition, and address any major gaps in your work history with a simple sentence in your summary section. And then move on.

Finally, as you look to leverage LinkedIn to return to work, build your profile and approach your job hunt with these guiding principles: Be transparent. Be authentic. Be confident. Good luck!

—Katie Fogarty, LinkedIn Reboot

The Old-Fashioned Résumé

Even though LinkedIn is a critical search tool and a required online presence for professionals, you still need an old-fashioned résumé that you can send out to employers seeking applicants. It's the standard calling card. Recruiters or managers might find you on LinkedIn and read your profile, but they're still going to request that you e-mail your résumé or upload it to their job application page for easy reference. And you'll need it when you apply for jobs through a company website or HR department. I have no doubt you'll be able to wow potential employers with your personality and fresh ideas once you get an interview, but your résumé is what's going to get you that interview. And it'll only have about six seconds in which to do it. Literally.

TheLadders.com reported that human resources professionals take an average of six seconds to review your résumé. In the first four seconds, they scan your job titles, previous employers, dates, and education. They glance at everything else in the remaining two. That's four to six seconds to impress the gatekeepers and convince them that they should spend fifteen more seconds e-mailing or calling you, not the other two hundred people whose résumés are in a digital pile below yours. That's not a lot of time. In fact, it probably took you longer than six seconds to read this paragraph. So your résumé needs to be killer—so well put together and so strong as to make people realize they'd be crazy not to hire you.

COMEBACK QUOTE

"As soon as you're thinking about returning, find a recruiter for your industry and send them your résumé with a request for feedback. They will either say, 'It's great, don't change a thing.' Or they'll tell you, 'This is outdated and needs to be reworked.' Recruiters know your market better than anyone else and you'll get immediate feedback."

—Mayda, publishing professional, mother of four

Getting Started

So how do you do it? How do you build a great résumé? Follow the directions below.

Limit it to one page. It's fine within reason to adjust the margins or play with fonts to fit everything you think is important onto one page, but remember that your résumé should look clean and be easy to read. White space is a good thing. It means that your reader can focus on the critical information without getting distracted by unnecessary clutter. Employers want to see résumés that can tell them at a glance whether it's worth putting yours in the contact file or the trash pile. It's possible that two- or three-page résumés are acceptable in some sectors, but make sure you investigate by talking to peers in your field and find out before submitting one.

Lead with a prominent header. Put your name, your contact information, and your LinkedIn profile connection at the top. Make them stand out. Believe it or not, some people won't look any further; they'll just go right to your social media sites to check you out from there. If your Twitter, Instagram, and Pinterest profiles are tied to your professional life or represent your work in some way, add those as well. You want to make it as easy as possible for someone to see your e-mail address or phone number so they can easily contact you.

Use a professional-sounding e-mail address. An unprofessional e-mail address likely won't get you in for an interview—in fact, according to a CareerBuilder.com survey, one third of the time an inappropriate e-mail address will get you rejected. So if your personal e-mail is currently *stacymom23@gmail.com*, open up a new, professional e-mail address that makes no reference to your mom status or your kids. *First.lastname@insertemailhere.com* is best, of course, but come up with a simple variation if someone else has already snagged your name.

Job objective. The first line below your header should be your job objective. It should only be one sentence long. For example: *Seeking a position as an administrative assistant in a financial services office.* Be thoughtful about your objective statement; it should be a powerful line describing exactly the job you want.

Professional accomplishments. Choose the most significant moments in your professional history, and include only the ones that pertain to the particular job you're applying for. You'll need only one bullet point to explain each. This is different from work experience, where you list two to three specific skills under each job position. These are three or four separate lines that showcase some of the bigger moments in your past career. For example: *Led a team of ten on a multichannel marketing campaign for a Fortune 500 company.* Choose your words carefully and make every single one count. You need to show that you have a great attitude, will work hard, and will bring new ideas to the table.

Work experience. This is brief. List your most recent job title, the name of the company where you worked, the city in which it was located, and the dates during which you worked there. Include one to three bullet-point descriptions of what you did, using strong action verbs. And remember, if you're applying for a job as an accountant, there's no need to include your experience as a waitress eight years ago.

Education. Unless you're a recent graduate and this is the first full-time job you've applied for, put this section at the bottom of the page. If you've been out of the game for a while, don't put the year in which you graduated. If you earned a significant and prominent scholarship, like a Rhodes or Fulbright, list it here.

Highlight your best self. Go ahead and mention your volunteer work in the accomplishments section if you can demonstrate metrics that show you conducted some successful, results-driven projects, efficacy, or initiative, such as:

- Led marketing team initiative that resulted in quantifiable increased exposure for after-school STEM program targeting disadvantaged girls ages eight to eighteen.

- Contributed to PR campaign that increased museum membership revenues for three consecutive quarters.

- Reduced neighborhood food-waste composting program costs by 17 percent.

- Reorganized the library at Sunnyside Elementary School, resulting in enough found space to fit two additional computer stations.

Definitely list your skills as logistics, accounting, or office management, whether those skills were attained at the job before you left the workforce, while running your household (without resorting to cutesiness—see Mom-Mistake #1 above), managing a charity, or volunteering at your house of worship. Don't hide the fact that you have a master's degree from Harvard and a PhD from Yale in the education section, even if the job you're applying for wouldn't need an applicant with such advanced degrees. Whatever makes you shine the brightest, put that first, because whoever's reading is only going to scan the page and may not even make it to the end—assuming it's a "who" doing the reading, and not a "what."

Include keywords. If you apply for a position at a large company, there is a strong chance that it won't be a human looking at your résumé. Many human resource departments now use what is known as "application tracking software," or ATS, to help them sift through hundreds of applications. According to an April 2015 article in *Forbes*, this software allows companies to electronically manage their recruiting and hiring process to store and track information about applicants.[17] It scans résumés for specific keywords related to the job posting. For example, if an employer insists that a candidate have experience in Excel, the computer will only flag résumés that include the word *Excel* for the callback list. While this process saves

---

17. Lisa Quast, "Why Resume Keywording Is a Must for Job-Seekers," *Forbes*, www.forbes.com/sites/lisaquast/2015/07127/why-resume-keywording-is-a-must-for-job-seekers/#69eb609a38e6.

time for employers and HR departments, it means that the résumés of promising applicants might get tossed out just because they don't have the right keywords.

There are lots of keywords moms could include on their résumés that would show what they could offer a company. You definitely exhibit "organizational leadership" if you did any volunteer work at your kid's school or spent time as a member of the PTA. And "multi-tasking" should definitely make its way somewhere onto your résumé. Ask yourself what types of traits and qualities you've developed or had to learn to be a mom. I encourage you to come up with five phrases or words that best describe who you are today, and your best traits and qualities, and find a way to work them into the skills section of your résumé.

But make sure those keywords match what your prospective employer is seeking. Look at the job listing or posting, and see if any of the keywords in the job description match your skills in some way. If there is not a formal job posting, take a look at the company's website, and go to the "about us" section on the page for a general description of the company's day-to-day operations, goals, and objectives. Use the same terms the company uses.

I reached out to some of my viewers recently to see if adding keywords to their résumé helped them land a job. The response was overwhelmingly positive:

I tweaked my résumé to use keywords from the job posting. I received three offers from doing it. –Andrew

I tweaked my résumé and ended up with an offer within a week. –Olaf

Additional materials. Some industries—for example, design, architecture, and advertising—require portfolios, samples, or visual documentation of your work. Talk to others in the industry to find out whether the requirements have changed since you were last in the workforce. In my field, people who produce shows build a reel to show prospective employers examples of some of the segments they've contributed to. Back in the not-too-distant past, that reel would have been on tape, but today everything has gone digital. Many people put their work up on websites. If you do, make sure that Web address is included on your résumé and connected to your LinkedIn profile.

Cover Letters

I'll never forget the first paper résumé I created in college, and the accompanying cover letter that I always included, which I then put in an envelope, attached a stamp to, and mailed out. That was then, and this is now, and the truth is that in most instances a cover letter is now known as the "cover e-mail you attach your résumé to." Other than the means of delivery, the same basic rules apply if you are e-mailing your résumé to a specific person at a company. You greet them by name and state who you are and the job you are applying for. Keep the message short, and make sure there is a call to action, such as "Do you have a few minutes to speak by phone about the position?" or "Do you have fifteen minutes to see me for an informational interview?" before you sign off. (That's the sneaky way of saying, I want the job, but hey, we're just chatting! No pressure.)

Finally, make sure there are *absolutely no typos* in your cover letter or résumé. You'd be surprised how many executives and HR people I speak to say they get résumés riddled with typos, poor grammar, and faulty punctuation. Read your work out loud. Proofread it. Then get someone else to proofread it. Check and triple check. According to CareerBuilder.com, 61 percent of recruiters will dismiss a résumé because of typos. You can't afford something stupid like a grammatical error to ruin your chances of landing an interview.

TEN RÉSUMÉ DOS

1. **Include language used in the job posting.** Since you're tailoring the résumé to a job, if the post says "must have strong managerial skills," use those words and explain how.

2. **List an objective.** Tell your potential future employer what you are seeking and what you can offer.

3. **Simplify.** Edit your résumé, especially in the work experience section. Use your words wisely and don't list every single thing you did in your previous jobs. Be succinct.

4. **Be agile.** Have two or three versions of your résumé and adjust and personalize each, depending on the job you're applying for. Make sure you check the job posting carefully and rewrite your résumé to best align with the skills required to land an interview.

5. **Be consistent.** Whatever style you choose to use for your résumé, be consistent. So if you're listing your former job by title, company, city, and date, do that for every single job. Don't put the company first for one and the city first for another. Be consistent in your use of boldface or italics, tense, and first or third person.

6. **Make it visually appealing.** Use the Arial font; keep it clean and formatted nicely.

7. **Include professional memberships.** This shows you're still active.

8. **Include volunteer work.** This shows you are civic minded and that reflects well on you.

9. **Update frequently.** Don't create your résumé and be done. You need to keep updating it constantly.

10. **Use bullet points.** Don't use long, ramblinging sentences. You're not writing *War and Peace*.

TEN RÉSUMÉ DON'TS

1. **Don't abbreviate anything.** Spell it all out using complete, adult words.

2. **Don't try to be funny.** No "I did ten beer bongs at my frat house."

3. **Don't put salary requirements.** If they want to talk money, they'll bring it up.

4. **Don't list past salaries.** You don't want to price yourself above the range an employer might have in mind, and you also don't want to underprice yourself. Also, you don't want to suggest that money is your only motivation.

5. **Don't list references.** Think of your résumé a little like a first date. You want the employer to call you back, so don't give everything away right away. If they like you, they'll call and ask for references, which will give you a chance to have another conversation and engage with them.

6. **Don't be fancy or artistic.** Don't design your résumé, don't add graphics, don't add art. Words only, preferably just a few.

7. **Don't lie or embellish.** There's a big difference between highlighting your strengths and making something up. Your résumé needs to be 100 percent truthful.

8. **Be smart about how you mention your kids or personal life.** List hobbies and interests *only* if they somehow apply to your professional life. Don't list your children's activities; this is about you only. If you must include personal information in your résumé, make it purposeful.

9. **Avoid TMI.** Don't make people uncomfortable.

10. **Don't use gimmicks or tactics.** No sending cakes to the office with your résumé tucked inside.

How Kylie Did It

Kylie had heard that once you stepped out of the workforce to have kids you could never get back in, but she was determined to buck that trend and beat the system. She'd done the New York corporate grind in finance. So when she did go back, she wanted it to be to an interesting yet low-pressure job that met all of her criteria: challenging work, decent pay, and flexible hours. Determined to win her way back in without compromise, she thought about her skills and interests and decided to make a radical career switch. She studied library sciences with the goal of becoming a librarian.

In school she performed well and found an encouraging adviser

who affirmed that she was on the right path and helped boost her frag-
ile confidence. Then the time came to start applying for jobs, but whenever she tried working on her résumé she still had the same old problem
staring her in the face: a five-year gap she needed to explain away. How
could she convince an employer to overlook her age and see that she
could do a better job than all those young recent graduates she was
competing against because she still had all the old skills she'd learned
in corporate America? She was paralyzed by the same issue when she
tried to fill out her profile on that new site LinkedIn that everyone told
her was so important. What could she possibly say there? She knew
she needed to find the appropriate language to describe what she had
done and what she was capable of, but in addition she somehow needed
to craft a story, a professional one, not one that revolved around her
kids. She had to figure out a way to explain how the skills and experience she'd earned from successful career number one would translate
to a successful career number two. Problem was, she had no clue how.

So she hired a professional, who was able to carefully craft the perfect narrative, one that revealed what she used to do as well as where
she wanted to go—avoiding highlighting her professional gap. Her
adviser was able to help her develop a story to explain why combining
her old skills in finance with her new training in library science made
sense, and that someone with that combination of knowledge and expertise would be a unique asset to anyone smart enough to hire her. By
focusing the story on everything she *had* done over the past few years,
the résumé adviser was able to gloss over what she hadn't. There was no
mention of those five blank years, rather a clear link between finance
and library science. Kylie's adviser boosted her résumé and LinkedIn
profile with value propositions. In addition, the adviser showed Kylie

that her career switch was actually a good thing, because it allowed her to present herself as a fresh product. Prospective employers would be likely to ignore the five-year gap because everything that came before it was pretty much irrelevant so long as Kylie could sell herself as someone perfectly qualified *right now* for the job they needed to fill. When Kylie finally landed a full-time job as a college librarian and instructor, it was a fulfilling and challenging position that paid her above the minimum she needed to earn and offered generous vacation time. And no pressure-cooker atmosphere. She had, in fact, beat the system.

Hiring a professional is an excellent option if you can afford it. Women often find it difficult to toot their own horns, but an objective party won't hesitate to tell the world why you're awesome. But of course, if you can't afford to hire a professional, don't let that stop you. Be bold. Pretend you're writing about a friend instead of about yourself. Would you hold back if you were trying to help someone you cared about get a job? Of course not, because you would want the world to see your friend the way you see her. Let the world see you the way you deserve to be seen.

5

Choose Your Moment

O nce you have made the decision to go back to work, reactivated your network, and have your résumé ready to go, there remains, of course, the $64,000 question: *When* will you go back? When will you be ready? What will be the right time to dive back in, both for your career and your family? You may not have a choice about timing, but if you do, you'll want to examine whether or not your children are ready (they probably are), give yourself a confidence boost, decide what kind of comeback moment you want, and then get ready to launch.

What About the Children?

More than anything else, most women interviewed for this book said that the thing that gave them pause and the most angst was concern over the effect their comeback would have on their children. Would the kids feel abandoned if they had to go to after-school care or a babysitter watched them in the afternoons? Would evenings become rushed and unpleasant because all the nighttime routines would have to be compressed into a shorter window before bedtime? Would their kids be at a disadvantage compared to the other kids whose moms stayed home?

COMEBACK QUOTE

"A lot of the decisions you make about returning to work depend on your partner and what kind of a job they have and what kind of hours they have. That impacts your babysitting arrangements. My husband is a great partner and we work together as a team. But he doesn't have a nine-to-five job. He works nights and during the busy season six or seven days a week. That meant when I assessed what I was going to do, I knew he couldn't be counted on. So that impacted how I approached my return."

—Doriana, TV producer, mother of two

It's worth noting that few of these women found that any of their worst nightmares materialized. In fact, the opposite was true—their kids adjusted very well and even learned some important lessons about family teamwork, self-sufficiency, and patience. Ultimately, it wasn't the kids who had a rough time with the transition, but rather some of the mothers as they came to terms with the loss of certain beloved routines, or the fact that they might sometimes have to miss school and sporting events. Sandra had never committed to dropping out of the workforce altogether, but it never occurred to her that one day she'd be working full time and raising her daughter. But once she realized financially that it was time to go back full time, she took pride in knowing her daughter was watching her mother step up, learning the meaning and importance of being independent, and fully understanding that women can achieve success. "It is important for me to have her know that she can do whatever she wants to do," Sandra said. "The definition of success is different for me than it will be for her, but I want her to have the confidence to know she can be who she wants to be." One additional lesson Sandra learned that she felt was important to pass on to her daughter: there may not always be 100 percent balance between work and home. "You can't have it all—not all at once." The scale tips one way or the other. The key: let it shift back and forth so it's not always on one side of the spectrum for too long.

Sandra's experience bears out what many studies have already established: children actually benefit from being raised by mothers who work outside the home. The following findings might ease any pain you may feel as you grapple with the impact your decision may have on your kids' futures.[18]

- Daughters of moms who work grow up to be more successful in the workplace than their peers. They make more money and they often end up being bosses.

- Sons of moms who work grow up to be dads who take a more active role with child care and chores in their households.

- The children of working moms grow up with a more egalitarian view on gender roles.

A lot of mothers I spoke with said that the anticipation of going back to work was harder than actually going to work. In fact, after

18. Carmen Nobel, "Kids Benefit from Having a Working Mom," Harvard Business School's *Working Knowledge* blog, http://hbswk.hbs.edu/item/7791.html.

a short period of time, most reported they were at peace with their decision, especially when they realized that they were not only acting as good role models, but also actually making their children proud. In the end, most said once they figured that out, they knew they'd done the right thing.

Give Yourself a Win

Concern about the impact their decision to go back to work will have on their children is not the only thing that slows down many women or makes them hesitate, perhaps longer than they should. It's a lack of confidence. It's a bit of a Catch-22, really. You need a win to feel good about yourself, but you don't think you can get a win because your skills are soft and you've been out for too long. My advice: dive in. Just making one connection or one new contact is a win. And when you make it, write it down. Maybe you'll only have one win per week for a while, but after a few weeks, it's likely you'll start noting daily wins—someone acknowledged receipt of your résumé or you found the perfect class to tune up your skills. Eventually, you'll have a list of twenty small wins, which will help you feel good. If you've been out for a while you may have to take baby steps. But trust me when I say that every little bit helps. The big win—the job or the job interview or even just the right job opportunity—will come.

Ann Mukherjee, global chief marketing officer at SC Johnson, is a mother herself and someone I've known for years. When it comes to being a mom and a successful and inspiring top executive, she seems to know how to make it work better than anyone else. Her job constantly takes her around the world for business, but every time I see her, she tells me how she always makes it a priority to set aside time on her calendar to take fun trips with her husband and children, and to make sure, no matter what, that she is home for the big events in their lives. She's also spoken to many women who have grappled with returning to the corporate world as they assessed what they would be giving up if they returned. She's heard them stress about whether they have a contribution that's worth making since they have been out for so long. She assures women that going back to work won't make their kids suffer. The opposite, in fact, is true: you'll grow and they'll grow. "Maybe you can't have it all every day, but you can have it over a lifetime."

Your workplace is going to benefit from you being there. You're going to feel like you've accomplished something huge. You're going to blossom in ways you didn't at home. Don't hold yourself back out of fear. Be bold. Remember the pre-kid you? Be her. Grab hold of whatever inspired her to chase a dream back in the day. You have a unique set of talents—be confident enough to use them, and make your decisions about timing with self-assurance.

Make a Plan A and a Plan B

In order to know if you and your family are ready, get out paper and a pen and develop two plans. Plan A will outline how it's all going to work. Plan B will outline how it's all going to work when plan A falls apart. Both plans should include contingency plans for:

Child care. Are the kids in school or must you hire help to stay home with them? Is there day care nearby or might there be one available where you eventually work? What's your partner's schedule and flexibility—are there blackout times that will impede his ability to step in? Does this impact the type of job you can take? Given that you don't know what job you'll have, use your best guess. Who will do pickup? Who will do drop-off? Who will make lunches? Who will make dinner? Who will stay home if a child gets sick? Who will attend parent/teacher conferences? If the kids are older, what's their mobility? Is a second or third car available to them to ease the burden? Chart out the obligations that pertain to your situation. What's realistic? What's not?

Commuting. How far are you willing to travel? Can you afford to spend one hour getting to work? Do you have only one car? Do you detest the train? Really assess all of these elements. Are you planning a move that could make your commute more difficult than it would be today?

Community obligations. Who will take over the Girl Scout troop? How will you get someone to take over for you as PTA treasurer? Who will organize the monthly fund-raising bake sale? Will you buy out of the required volunteer hours at your child's school? Who will take your place on Tuesdays at the food pantry?

Knowing you have a plan and a backup plan should help you feel more organized, more secure, and more confident when you start looking for work.

Write Down Your Goals

A great way to figure out when to make your comeback is to look far into the future and write down how you want to get there. Keep a back-to-work journal to record all of your leads, contacts, and concerns in one place. That will help you assess how current you are and whether or not reconnecting will impact the timing of your return. If you like a notebook, great, use that. If you want to use a computer file, that works, too. Now, where do you see yourself personally and professionally in five years? What about ten? What are your financial goals? How much time will you need in the workforce to help you meet them? Must you jump in now or much later? Map out the path to meeting these goals and you'll have a ballpark idea of what your timing should be.

Maybrooks.com, a website for working moms, has an actual tool kit online to help you assess if you're ready to jump back in. Take a look at it.

Leave Yourself Enough Time

Maybe you think you'll be ready to start your comeback in one year. If that's the case, remember that you'll actually want to start sooner. Start before you need to start; you will need time to get organized and make sure you're ready to start applying for jobs. You'll need time to make sure your rebrand is successfully complete. You don't want to wait until you're financially up against a wall before you start looking.

The good news, though, is that even if you have to move faster than is ideal, you will be fine. Your children will be fine. You are a smart, accomplished woman, and being a mom will have taught you how to flex. Plan your timing as best you can, and then work with whatever comeback works with the resources you have. What kind of comeback will you launch? We'll discover that in the next chapter.

Part II

Launching Your

Comeback

6

Choose the Comeback That's Right for You

J ust because your ultimate goal should be to build a career doesn't mean you have to jump into the workforce full time right away. You may need to or want to, but it's OK to take a gradual approach, too. In fact, dipping your toes in slowly, one foot at a time, can often be an excellent way to give yourself some time to gain the experience or confidence you need to take the next big leap.

I like to take the most direct route to get from A to D to get a story on the air. But when searching for a job, take the path that gets you where you want to be. That might not be the path you expected to take. In fact, where you think you want to be might end up being somewhere else completely. There are opportunities everywhere in places we often never think to look.

You may decide to return to the exact position that you left. You may move to a similar position at a different company. Some women change industries altogether, and others find themselves starting lower on the totem pole and working their way up. Depending on your circumstances, a nontraditional path like volunteering or interning might be the launching point of your comeback. Or maybe you'll even launch your own business. Your next step should be to understand all the opportunities available to you.

Assess Your Career History

Look back at the choices you've made in your life. This will be easier if you've just completed your résumé. When you graduated from college, did you take the first job you were offered? Did you have ambitions of doing something else but got scared and therefore took the bird in the hand? I switched careers from flight attendant to television news reporter because I knew what I wanted to do in my heart, but I took a long time before making that change. But some of you probably graduated, took a job, succeeded at it, took another job in that field, and then voilà—a career was made by inertia. What if you could do it all again, would you make different choices? Maybe you were on the wrong path to begin with?

Maybe once you sit down and assess your skills, hopes, and plans you'll be able to look at this return to work post-baby as a do-over—an opportunity rather than a burden. Then again, maybe you nailed it the first time around, landed right where you were supposed to be, and now you're ready to get back to it. Just make sure to ask yourself: Is that gig still compatible with my life with kids? Some women will be very fortunate and find that they can return to something exactly like or very similar to what they left. And some will have to—or choose to—return to something related to what they were doing before, but not exactly the same thing.

CAREER EXPERTS SAY

"One of the biggest mistakes that [I actually] made myself when I relaunched my own career after eleven years out of the full-time workforce was failing to do a career assessment. We think it's very important to step back and reflect on whether your interests and skills have changed or have not changed while you have been on career break. The longer you've been out, the more important it is."

—Carol Fishman Cohen, iRelaunch

Carol Fishman Cohen at iRelaunch has her clients make a plan before diving back in, but not everyone has the luxury of doing so. Many moms can't take the time to be strategic because time isn't on their side or finances are dire. If this is you, all is not lost. According to Fishman Cohen, it's fine if you need to buy yourself time with any old job. Use your evenings to plan for the next career move, for the second gig that will be your true comeback. Being strategic about getting to your next career will make it much more likely that you wind up working in a job that is in line with your current interests, skills, and lifestyle.

Identify Your Skill Set

Hilary once held a big job in New York publishing as a marketer and branding expert. When she left the field to spend more time with her firstborn, she was working exclusively on a desktop computer and using an early version of the BlackBerry. Twitter didn't even exist, and neither did Instagram. Two children and a move to London later, she decided to return to the workforce even though her plate was full with the house, a new country as home, and kids; she was ready for a "little twitch of stress" that would keep her active and thinking about other things in the world besides her children's grades or her next dinner party.

She decided she would not return to publishing, not because she didn't love it, but because she had left on a high note, and she was sure that she could not perform at that level again, for now anyway. "I didn't even for a moment consider going back into publishing because I felt that I couldn't re-create what was so exceptional about the times I had [there.]" She would have to reinvent herself.

So she tackled the search for something new by creating a list of skills, including all that she had learned from publishing, managing events, doing PR, and placing magazine pieces, as well as what she'd taken away from the volunteer activities in which she'd immersed herself while she was a stay-at-home mother. Rather than hiding the fact that she'd taken a break, she used smart, active language on her résumé to highlight the challenges of the work she had taken on while at home. (No padding or exaggeration was necessary, she said: "Being president of the PTA was the hardest thing I've ever done.") And then she started hunting for jobs that would appeal to her interests and best utilize her skills.

All her efforts helped her land a gig in marketing with a small fitness company (fitness being one of Hilary's passions), running a team whose members were all about fifteen years her junior.

Hilary was smart enough to realize that she couldn't go back to what she'd done before, and brave enough to try something new. When you transition careers you have to be ready to shift and reinvent yourself. Make a list to help you identify your priorities and your goals. What's changed since you last worked? What's different in your life? How will work fit into it? List what you know, whom you know, and what you don't know but need to learn. Can you revive your once-vibrant career life, or has the landscape changed so much it won't be the same great experience for you again? How much have *you* changed? Will you gain the same satisfaction from that kind of work that your old self did? The answers will help you assess where to target your job search.

Don't Act Out of Desperation

If you assess your career history and skills and believe you can step right back into your old track, that's wonderful. If you can't, don't freak out and, above all, don't act out of desperation. Desperation can compel you to make mistakes. You're not desperate even if you think you are; you don't have to take the first thing that comes along. If you need cash quickly, sure, take what you can get, but never lose sight of the fact that it's just a stopgap, a temporary place to land where you can earn money while taking the necessary steps to get to your real career, the one that will give you the gratification and the pay you want.

The good news is that you might not have to take a bad stopgap job if you plan carefully. Maybe your schedule won't allow you to maintain the hours of your old job, but that doesn't mean you have to settle for something terrible. Rachael Ellison, a career coach and work/life advocate, often works with serious type-A career women who gave 150 percent to their former careers and had planned to reach a level of seniority by a certain age, only to discover that now that they have small children they can't give their jobs the same energy and undivided focus. The solution, according to Ellison, is not to give up on your career, but to learn a different way to demonstrate your value. You have two choices:

- Pivot: Change from an incompatible field to a more family-friendly one.

- Rethink: Talk to management and discuss how you could get work done in a way that works for both parties. Some companies are up for it, some aren't. Choosing the right one when you go back to work will make all the difference.

EXERCISE: PIVOT OR RETHINK?

You've decided it's time to go back to work, but you have been out for so long you have no idea what you intend to do or what career to pursue. With Ellison's assistance I created this exercise to help you identify your unique skill set. It will help you sort through what you'd like to learn to move into a job and will help you assess the skills you have acquired while out that can translate into professional and marketable.

Step One: Take Inventory of Your Experiences

Write down what you've been doing and the skills that you have developed while you have been a stay-at-home mom. What skills are marketable? Were you involved in community activities? How could those activities translate?

Step Two: What Speaks to You?

Make a list of companies, sectors, organizations, and jobs whose culture speaks to you, even if only as a consumer. Why do you like these organizations or positions? What about them appeals to you and your values and insights? Now, write down what your dream job might be if you were deciding for the very first time on a career path. Then compare—is your dream job aligned in any way with the culture of a sector or company? Could you see that job existing at that company?

Now, narrow down the list if there are matches.

Step Three: What's Most Important to You?

This one is important since it's fair to say that everything in life is a trade-off. What can you live with, what can you compromise on, and what is most critical to you? Some things to consider:

Convenience

Daily Responsibilities

Commute

Hours

Money

Step Four: Target

Now find specific companies that meet the criteria from your list and target them.

How do they match your mind-set and priorities?

Would the commute, money, and/or hours work well for you and be a good fit?

Once you've made that list, you might be able to shorten and tighten it so you know exactly whom to target and why. There's no point in wasting your time on companies that ultimately won't work for you and your goals.

If you find you just need to rethink, congratulations. The odds are good that you'll be able to find something workable with your boss. If you find you need to pivot, congratulations to you, too! You're about to begin an exciting adventure.

I love what I do for a living, and I got there because of a pivot—not a motherhood pivot, but a pivot nonetheless. When I decided to make the switch into broadcasting, it wasn't because I didn't want to be a flight attendant anymore; it was because I wanted to work in television news. I knew what I wanted, I followed my gut, and I made a plan. I did an internship at a television station during the week, and worked with the airline on the weekends to pay my rent while living in San Francisco. I did what I needed to do to get the career I wanted. That is where you are right now. You're not just going for a job—your goal should be a career. Because it's only worth it to give up stay-at-home motherhood if you're giving it up for a career that you love and in which you can succeed and thrive.

Be Creative

While you don't want to take a job you hate if you don't have to, you may find yourself needing to be creative if you're going to need to pivot. The good news is that if you're flexible, there are more options out there for moms entering new fields than ever before. Whether you decide to volunteer, intern, or even start your own business, you have options.

Volunteering

Karyn and her husband were both in the military, but she stopped working when she realized that their constant moves around the world made it impossible for her to continue her career and take care of their two children. She never intended to rejoin the workforce, despite having earned a degree specializing in public relations. When cracks in the marriage began to appear, Karyn started to look for employment, knowing divorce was likely on the horizon. But she soon realized she had shot herself in the foot. After serving in the Navy and then seven years as a stay-at-home mom, she had no résumé. No contacts. No network. Nothing.

She briefly tried to find paying work, but none of her Navy experience or skills were transferable to the types of jobs she was applying for, plus this was 2001, and none of the programs now offered to veterans were in existence. In addition to that, she had given up her military job to become a military spouse, so she could take care of the children while her husband was sent on several deployments. Even if the military offered assistance, as a spouse at that time, she didn't qualify. Add to all of this the fact that being with kids for so long was held against her. A few prospective employers made comments suggesting she had done the right thing for her family, but most focused on the gap and what she had *not* achieved. Once she was even told, "This is not the kind of job you want as your first job, going back. There's a lot of travel. Maybe it's not for a new mom coming back to the workforce."

She knew she could get work at a department store, but she wanted a career in public relations, not a job. So she researched for hours and hours to figure out a path in. Eventually, she decided to step back, be more targeted in her search—seeking out companies with clients that might need Washington or military connections in some way—and then offer her services as a volunteer with the hope that the company would be impressed with her work and hire her. It took her a very long time, but eventually after finding the right firm and volunteering for several months, she landed a full-time job. While volunteering was a financial hardship at first, Karyn felt that it set her up to be paid $25,000 a year more than she would have gotten going in had she started at entry level without the volunteer work on her résumé. Karyn treated that internship as a full-time job in her mind, and gave it the same dedication she would give to a paid position. The bosses noticed, and not only was she scooped up by the firm, she rose within the ranks faster than most. It was a win-win for both.

You're Never Too Old for an Internship

Not everyone is able to take advantage of the opportunities offered through internships, but for those who are, they can be a great way to get your foot in the door, to get references, and even to prove yourself to people making the hiring decisions. Internships can also be work-arounds—on-the-job training for those who can't afford or can't spend the years it would take to get another degree if that's what's necessary to get a position in your chosen field.

I have firsthand experience that this strategy can work. When I decided to switch from the airline industry into television news, rather than pursue a graduate degree in journalism, I enrolled in a couple of community college courses so that I would be eligible for a spring internship at the CBS affiliate in San Francisco. To supplement my income and pay my bills, I continued to work as a flight attendant for Southwest Airlines on weekends. Yes, I worked seven days a week for six months during that internship. However, my reduced hours at the airline hurt my bank account, and I did accrue debt. Learn from my mistake in that regard, and think ahead of time about your financial plan!

I maxed out that time, maybe because I was older than the rest of the interns. I'd already had life experience and knew what I wanted. I was driven. I used the internship to make my tape, go out on shoots, and soak up all of the news experience I could get. Ultimately, that station offered me a job as a production assistant, but I *also* got offered a job producing for a national travel show, which led to an opportunity to be in front of the camera. I was honest when I sat down for the job interview, and that was key. When I was asked by the interviewer "What is your ultimate goal?" I said I'd eventually like to be a reporter. His response was "Well, we'll see." You should know I held him to those words, begging and pleading for several weeks for any opportunity, because my ultimate goal was to be in front of, not behind, the camera. That travel show was broadcast across the country, so eventually he said yes, and my first segment as a reporter aired nationwide—pretty good for a former flight attendant.

I realize that what might be feasible at the age of twenty-seven isn't always at age thirty-eight or forty-seven or fifty-one, and that the older you are, the harder it might be to accept the idea of taking an internship, especially an unpaid one. But while many companies like interns for their free labor and the extra help they offer around the office, they also use internships to handpick their next up-and-comers.

In addition, the world is changing and some companies are seeing the value of giving older people a second chance and teaching them from within. Instead of being for inexperienced workers, these new midlife internships (or, as Goldman Sachs calls their program, "returnships") are designed for midcareer professionals who have been out of work for a couple of years. And they are perfect for mothers who have a gap in their résumé.[19]

Megan, for example, had worked in the district attorney's office and been general counsel for an Internet company before taking eight years off to raise her children. She felt severely out of the loop. When an executive at Goldman Sachs reviewed her résumé and said, "There's this huge gap in your résumé, but tell me what you did all these years," Megan realized she needed to think harder about how she could present and leverage her eight years of child-raising experience. When she heard about a program at Credit Suisse called Real Returns, a paid internship for women getting back into the workforce after a gap, she reworked her résumé to leverage what she had done at home. "When you think about it," Megan said, "[as] a stay-at-home-mom—moving my kids to Europe, getting them into schools there, being involved with the school, and fund-raising—I was using my skills even if I wasn't in an actual paid job." So Megan created a job title to help her land a competitive slot at the bank: "domestic executive." She wanted to fill that previously apparent gap by leveraging her organizational skills, her ability to project-manage, and

---

19. Anne Tergesen, "Internships for 40-somethings Take Root on Wall Street," *Market-Watch*, http://www.marketwatch.com/story/internships-for-40-somethings-take-root-on-wall-street-2015-03-03.

how she'd coordinated the schedules of three children and all that came with that.

It worked. Megan landed a ten-week paid internship, along with several other people ranging in age from thirty to fifty. She loved everything about it—the group she worked with, the training, and the work itself, which was real project-based, compelling stuff. It helped her get back into the flow of working, and while it was challenging to adjust to the long days and kid-juggling, she said it was worth it.

What Megan gained in addition to landing a job:

- Confidence knowing that if she left the internship, she could interview and land a job elsewhere

- Access to insightful guest speakers and seminars

- Help with résumé writing and practice interviews

Getting your foot in the door isn't the only benefit of internships. They give you a chance to try a job on for size. Megan said some people in her program learned that they simply weren't ready to go back to work yet. If you intern somewhere and change your mind about returning to work, or decide you're not quite ready for it, but might be someday, or realize that this isn't the field for you, you haven't lost much time, nor burned any bridges or left anyone in the lurch.

MAKE SURE YOUR COMPANY PUTS ITS MONEY WHERE ITS MOUTH IS

"Think long and hard before taking an unpaid internship. Paid internships demonstrate a company's seriousness about bringing newbies along and getting them ready for full-time work."

—Megan, attorney, three children

Landing an Internship

In the age of Google, finding companies that are willing to train adults looking to change careers or reenter the workforce is fairly easy to do on the Internet. But before you start you need to identify some key things for yourself:

- What industry do you want to work in?

- Are you looking to make a complete change? If the answer is yes, identify the industry, then go to one of the financial websites that lists complete company information. I have always liked Yahoo! Finance. It groups companies by industry such as banking, industrial, retail, software developer, or energy production.

- If you can think of one company you might be interested in working for, under its details page on Yahoo! Finance, you'll also find other companies in their sector. Under each company listing you will find the address, website, and subsidiary information for the corporation.

- If you're finding that most internships require applicants to be students, enroll in a community college or take some online courses if they will allow you to qualify as a student.

Get Proactive

Pick up the phone. Yes, I said it, *the phone*. Call the main number and asked to be transferred to someone in human resources. Depending on the size of the company, you may get an actual person, on whom you will practice the cold-calling skills you learned in chapter 3. If you don't get a person on the phone, then it's time to draft an e-mail or apply online. If there is no internship application online, then you will need to write a short, specifically worded e-mail (which is what you should aim for with your cold call, too, by the way):

"Dear _____,

"My name is _____ and I'd like to inquire about a possible adult internship (not for a college student) with your company. I have been out of the workforce for the last xx years and am looking to get back into the xyz industry."

Remember, this is about honesty. Your résumé will have a gap, and you cannot hide that information, but no need to expand heavily on it in the introductory e-mail.

Create Your Own Internship

If you are dying to work for a company but you don't quite have the qualifications for an entry-level position, and it doesn't offer an adult internship program, you might try to create an internship for yourself. The first step will be to identify the company's needs. Go to the job postings section on their website and look at the current openings. Take a look at the requirements for each position that interests you. You probably don't have that particular skill set, but that's OK. Draft an e-mail or letter to the head of human resources and lay out a proposal for an adult internship. Explain your interest in their company and that though you know that even though you don't necessarily have the corporate work experience they want yet, you possess some of the qualities they want in a model employee, like motivation, drive, organizational skills, being a self-starter, and the ability to multitask. How do I know that's what they want? Because I see a lot of job descriptions and those words almost always show up. Highlight the ones you possess in your proposal. However you sell yourself as a worthwhile bet to a potential employer—in person, on the phone, in writing—demonstrate your ability to learn, your eagerness to develop new skills, and your enthusiasm for a new opportunity.

PLACES TO LOOK

Goldman Sachs trademarked the term *returnship* in 2008 to describe its ten-week paid return-to-work program, and many companies are now following their lead. British bank Barclays is working on a similar program in the UK; JPMorgan Chase, Credit Suisse, MetLife, and

Morgan Stanley are all in the process of developing or currently offer these programs. In fact, as I write this book, more industries are looking to launch similar programs, because the banks have been so successful getting moms and military veterans in particular back into the workforce.

The nationally recognized OnRamp Fellowship program places experienced female attorneys in law firms across the country.

Zillow, the real estate firm, recently started an internship program for a handful of computer scientists.

Questions to Ask Yourself Before You Take an Unpaid Internship

- Can you afford to work for free?

- Are the commute and hours required reasonable for an unpaid position, or at least worth the exposure and experience you'll gain?

- Will you be able to perform at your peak capacity?

- Is this internship meant to fill a gap on your résumé so you can apply elsewhere, or are you gunning for a gig within the company? Know your goal.

In Your Favor

Many companies are recognizing that having women among their ranks gives them an edge. Diversity provides opportunities for fresh perspectives and different opinions, which can often increase innovation and problem solving, and many managers are frustrated that they lose so much good talent when their female employees leave to raise children. So a lot of companies are interested in encouraging moms to test the waters and are actively working to ease the stress of starting anew by launching structured programs to get them in the door. The fact that these programs exist at all should calm your nerves when applying for internships, whether paid or unpaid.

CAREER EXPERTS SAY

"In the senior ranks, the retention of females has not been as strong. There is a keen industry focus on diversity to attract experienced women back into the workplace and an untapped talent pool to meet that opportunity."—Lisa Monaco, vice president and global program manager, Credit Suisse

"The company is hoping that these interns are the right match for the company and that the job JPMorgan Chase is offering is the job that person wants. The internship is a great opportunity to test that out."—Julie Lepri, JPMorgan Chase managing director

An unpaid internship isn't for everyone, and if there is any chance that you can get good experience or up to date in your industry in a paying position, you should take it. If you have a previous job on your résumé that will lend itself to a paid position, then by all means, don't do an adult internship. Only take an unpaid internship if it's the only way to get where you want to go, and if it's an ultrastrategic move. It really should be reserved for people who wish to change careers completely.

Remember, unless you're able to find a friend or family member to step in, you'll have new child-care expenses to pay while you're making your comeback. That can be a tough pill to swallow when you're working for little, and it's downright bitter if you're working for nothing.

And moms, if you get a student internship or one that isn't specifically for older professionals, and you find yourself surrounded by kids half your age, whatever you do, don't stress about it. Just get in there and explore any opportunities available to you. Remember, I was twenty-seven years old when I interned at the CBS affiliate in San Francisco. In television, that's ancient—way too old to be starting out. The other interns were young college students or recent grads. But while they were outside smoking pot, I was slaving away inside working on stories, cutting tape, tracking my voice over existing stories the station was producing, and begging the photographers to shoot my "stand-ups," where I would report the story in front of the camera. I knew I needed a résumé reel, and I also knew I was never going to convince a station somewhere to hire me as a reporter if all I had under my job history was "flight attendant." I needed the skills and the experience, and I had neither. But against the odds I got the job I wanted, and you can, too.

By the way, none of my fellow interns had job offers that spring, and I had two at the end of my six months.

Part Time: The Perfect Balance

Part-time work can be ideal for some moms. It's the closest thing to "balance" they can get, giving them a chance to use their professional experience and education, as well as earn income, while still getting more time with the kids than a regular full-time job would allow.

Don't Be Afraid to Make a Proposal

If you're still in the workforce and sure you want to step off the career path for a while to be home with the kids, consider talking to your employer about the possibility of working part time before walking away from the job entirely. Write a well-thought-out proposal that answers the following questions.

- What would part time look like? Would you work every day for a few hours, or just three full days a week? Could you work from home and in the office? Could you set your own hours so long as the work got done?

- What would the benefits to the company be? You will need to make a list of how it best serves *them* in this scenario (e.g., preservation of intellectual capital).

- What would the metrics be? What would you promise to accomplish, what would be your goals, and how would your new status boost the company's bottom line? Sell them on this.

- How can technology help?

Also look carefully at your maternity leave documentation. Remember Stacey, from chapter 2? Under a section in her paperwork titled "If You Choose Not to Return to Work" was a paragraph stating that after maternity leave, an employee could indeed return on a part-time basis and ensure her job was safe. You may find that you are also eligible for a part-time position if you want one; always read the fine print.

Job Sharing

Another form of part-time work is job sharing. Doriana had an interesting vantage point: in the 1990s she was a local news reporter who did story after story about companies making allowances for two working parents. Some were doing great things to accommodate their employees, such as offering flexible hours, which at the time was a new phenomenon. When she became pregnant and realized that she wanted to keep working, but not full time, she decided to get creative. She did some research, found a partner at work to team up with, and then came up with a plan. She proposed a job share—two people would cover one job. She did all the math to provide the company with evidence that having two people covering one job wouldn't cost them any more money. In fact, the way she framed it, she was giving them a chance to save money. Without the arrangement, neither woman would have stayed on, so the company was glad to find a way to preserve the brainpower and experience of two smart, competent employees, instead of having to spend resources finding and training two new ones. Doriana and her colleague pioneered something new at their company and set an excellent precedent for all the other moms who followed.

If you're interested in this option, consult with others who might have done it in the past, meet with human resources to see if it's a viable path, then write a concrete outline of how the job could be filled, handled, and paid for with two bodies in one seat. Even if your company has never done it before, don't be afraid to at least ask about it. In building your case:

- Do all the research for the company.

- Call other companies and find out what programs they have in place, or talk to other moms at other companies and find out what arrangements they've been allowed to negotiate.

- Lay out all the evidence that your plan, whatever it is (flex hours, job sharing, one day at home), won't cost the company money.

- Prove your suggestion can maintain and even improve productivity (maybe without commuting time one day a week you can work a longer day).

- Make sure it works for your sector. Doriana knew that in news, the reporting was very day-driven, which worked in her favor: so as long as someone was there to cover it, the job got done. If your job has more longer-term, face-to-face-type projects, then your plan must take that into account.

You simply never know if your boss will bite unless you ask. If you are a smart, valuable member of the team, and especially if you've been at the company a long time, it's in the company's best interest to hold on to that investment. It will cost them fewer dollars and headaches to keep you on board in any capacity than to hire and train someone entirely new.

Had Doriana not come up with a plan, she would have quit her job decades ago and found something else. That job-share program allowed her to keep a gig that she loved for years. Today, she's the news director.

Part-Time Beware

Part-time work does have its pitfalls—so be aware of what could go wrong. Many women have had great experiences, but several I spoke to were sucked into more work than they bargained for for half the pay. Some coaches say not to do it—not to go part time for that reason. But if you know your industry and you know how it works, you might be fine. Malory was not.

When Malory left her legal career for five years to raise her three kids, she never planned to return. Unfortunately, the market for her husband grew uncertain, and Malory realized that to protect her family she needed to change her plans. Realizing that it would take a few years to get back in the door, she started laying the groundwork before she actually needed the work. She faced several challenges, however:

- She'd let her connections go cold. All of them.

- The company she'd left, where she had been chief legal counsel, had been hit hard by the recession and was a shell of its former self.

- She and her family had moved out of Manhattan to Connecti-
  cut, where there were far fewer job opportunities. Yet she
  was determined to work close to home.

- She had let her license expire, further narrowing her options.

- Her in-house legal expertise had been in technology—
  technology that had changed at the speed of light in the five
  years she'd been away.

Malory went about her job search methodically. She knew she no
longer had the experience to attract a large company, so she targeted
small ones instead. Finally, on LinkedIn, she found a job posting that
sounded perfect: "A part-time council, sole council, to this small growing company . . . services, not technology." The company was based
in India, which was actually a plus, since Malory had worked with
Indian companies at her last job and was used to working with the
time zone difference and cultural differences. And the schedule—
three days a week, one to two days in the city—seemed ideal. Yes, it
would be a substantially smaller paycheck than the one she'd once
brought home, but she knew she would have to compromise to get the
flexibility that was so important to her. She interviewed for the position and got it. The job sounded too good to be true, and as it turned
out, it was.

Even though she had researched the culture of the company and
had all the stipulations of her part-time agreement in writing, things
didn't play out as expected. Malory was clear when she took the gig:
she would work three days a week. But in the end she worked much

more than that. In fact, ultimately, she was working full-time hours for part-time pay, both from home and on extra days in the office. When she did finally upgrade to full time, her pay increase was small, if not dismal, because she had no leverage. Because she'd undervalued herself, she ended up making a fraction of what she could have been earning elsewhere had she simply jumped in full time initially. She wants moms to know that the payoff of part time is not always worth the financial sacrifice.

Many of the women I spoke to told me that working part time didn't always mean part time. In fact, it rarely did. Though they were often physically at their desks two days a week, they were on call almost all the rest of the time. It was tough to balance for many. The one upside to part-time work today versus decades ago is that technology at least allowed them to be away from the office, giving moms a virtual office in the palms of their hands. Some felt the trade-off was worthwhile; others felt they were paid for part time but worked more than part time.

Temping

Dolores didn't think she'd have any trouble finding work. A Harvard-educated attorney, she had left the workforce in 2009 to have two children. Five years later, a divorce forced her back to work. Her credentials and license were still in order, and she was sure her experience as a formerly high-ranking attorney at a major financial firm was still relevant. After all, it had only been five years.

She started applying for jobs at the same senior level she had left, but she could not find anything. First, there weren't as many open posts at that level as she'd expected there would be. Second, firms were filled with in-house candidates lining up for the jobs she wanted. Finally, after months and months of spinning her wheels, she shifted gears and accepted a six-month temp position as a contractor at an investment bank.

Dolores felt demoralized. She had a law degree from Harvard, and she was a temp. It was such a step down, and the trajectory back to her former professional standing seemed impossibly steep. What she didn't realize at the time, though, was that even if it was only as a temp, Dolores had already achieved half the battle in making a successful comeback—*she'd gotten her foot in the door*. Who cares how she'd done it? What mattered was what she did once she got there. And she did something great.

One weekend while she was still relatively new to the company, Dolores was brought in to a project that needed tax and legal technical expertise. The first meeting was on a conference call. Dolores had never met any of the people on the line. As the call ensued, an issue came up that she knew how to address. Without stopping to think about her temp status, she jumped in and gave an entire rundown of her approach, explaining the issues and how she could tackle them. All of a sudden, a man interrupted and said, "I'm sorry. Who is this talking?" Dolores panicked. She'd said too much. She quietly explained she was the contractor. That she was new. Nothing could prepare her for the man's response: "I had to pause because that was the most articulate, well-reasoned soliloquy I've heard in the ten years I've been here. I just needed to know who you were."

She now refers to that call as the best day of her life.

Dolores was so overqualified for her position that she performed well above expectations. Translation: She was noticed immediately as a result. The entire project landed on Dolores's plate, and she ran with it. Had she not taken the gig that was offered, however low on the ladder it felt at the time, she wouldn't have had the chance to shine. Had she performed *as expected* in a higher-level gig, she might have blended in with the furniture. Instead, she killed it, far exceeding what she was brought in to accomplish.

As a result of her temping success, six months later she was accepted into a prestigious internship at the firm that accepts only ten people per year, out of a pool of about ten thousand applicants. It was designed for people coming back to work after a gap. It was an opportunity that would have led to much bigger things, like a managing director job. Incredibly, however, before Dolores could complete her program, a great job at another firm opened up, and she applied for and got the position. While she felt terrible about jumping ship for a full-time gig, the people she'd worked for at the temp firm were happy she'd landed something so significant and well suited to her strengths.

Don't be afraid to accept temp work as you get back out there. As long as you play your cards wisely, a temporary gig can be a great stepping-stone to your new career. Temp agencies enter into contracts with companies to help them find personnel to fill either short- or long-term positions. Most agencies specialize in a particular field such as accounting, office administration, construction, or technology. The best strategy is to do a search on Yelp for local staffing agencies that operate in your area. Just like real estate is hyperlocal, so is temp work. If you can pinpoint the major industries that operate in your community, you can likely find a local agency to which they outsource their temporary staffing.

DOLORES'S TAKEAWAY: EVERY JOB, NO MATTER HOW SMALL, IS AN OPPORTUNITY TO SHINE

- A lower-ranking position will give you the opportunity to get noticed.
- Speak up on calls and in meetings even if you're in a junior position. Be heard. Be confident.
- Take on projects you can succeed at even if they're beyond your pay grade.
- Don't play office politics while proving yourself. Head down, do the work. Period.
- Rebuilding your career to what it was BC might mean starting at a lower level than the one you once left, *and that's OK*.
- Don't undersell yourself, but don't waste a year seeking the unattainable. Keep doors open and consider all of your options, even if they're not quite what you want.
- Your desk might be piled with tasks you once considered beneath you. Execute with the same level of quality and apply the same work ethic you did before you left.
- Be prepared to work extra hard to prove yourself—you'll live up to your potential given the chance. You're used to doing *everything* at home. Just do that at work, too.
- Juggle fast, stay calm, and hide any exhaustion. Focus on the positive and keep working.

Online Jobs

One of the most common questions I get from viewers of all ages is, what type of work can I do from home? First, a big caveat about this.

Be careful! When I started doing research on this topic a few years ago, I found there were *a lot* of scams out there. If anyone asks you to pay them for initial training or setup fees, don't do it. Period.

Computers, Skype, FaceTime, and programs like Google Share, where you can share documents with people remotely over the Internet, have led to an entirely new job title: virtual personal assistant. These tech platforms manage the schedules, air travel, corporate event planning, or other tedious duties that movers and shakers don't have time to do. Other legitimate and virtual gigs include transcription, online teaching, data entry, and bookkeeping work.

Become an Entrepreneur

Many women who can't find the perfect job or want complete control over their work life go into business for themselves and are wildly successful. In this day and age, social media and the web have allowed mothers to create markets from scratch like never before. Entrepreneurship is perhaps the most challenging kind of comeback, but it's also potentially one of the most rewarding.

Susan left practicing law to raise a family. The decision was easy—with five kids and a busy husband, staying home felt like the logical thing to do. While Susan volunteered "a ton," as she put it, outside of the home as the kids were growing up, she was still micro-focused on her children's lives—so much so that when her oldest went off to college she was a complete mess, devastated and sad that the family would never live again under one roof as a unit. She took it so hard that eventually she realized that she needed to create a healthy distance from them and find something significant to do. "I had to have something else in my life. I used to tell my kids 'No pets, no plants.' I only did kids. Then it started to be that that wasn't as true. I needed something else."

Instead of going back to work as a lawyer, Susan created what she called "a jobby." It was an idea that started as a hobby, then slowly evolved into a job, that eventually led her to become the founder, owner, and editor in chief of her own business, *Your Teen Media*, a parenting resource. It flourished, growing into a booming family business.

The payoff: At her fiftieth birthday dinner, the family took turns around the table saying something nice about their mom. When Susan's oldest daughter said how proud she was that Susan had started a business, it was the greatest birthday gift Susan could have received.

In this digital age, it's super easy to hang out a shingle with a Facebook page or an actual website and consult or create a product and become an entrepreneur. The work to make the business viable takes effort, of course, but that shouldn't scare off any mom. First of all, you're no stranger to hard work—you're raising kids, after all. Second, you wouldn't generally start a business unless you were pretty passionate about the product or service you were selling. And finally, it's a lot more appealing to give your all to a business when the fruits of your hard work go directly to you and your family, not some corporation.

Social media has opened up a whole new world for entrepreneurs, giving them access to possible clients without ever having to leave their living room. And there's a virtual workforce out there to help you sweat the small stuff. You can outsource everything from accounting to business cards to web design with a quick Google search. You can even hire a virtual or remote assistant.

Start Early

Erin always loved photography, but when she studied it in college she took to heart the words of her professor: It's difficult to make a living as a photographer. So she didn't try to. Instead, she went into news and worked as a reporter. She continued to take photography classes and dabble in the darkroom, but it was always just for fun, on the side. When she left the workforce to raise two kids, she continued with her hobby, taking pictures of her children in the urban settings of Brooklyn. Eventually, noticing her skill and unique style, her friends started asking her to take their photos. And suddenly, Erin Turner Photography was born.

She had never thought of herself as a businesswoman, and sometimes she felt like she was in over her head. As she slowly transitioned out of stay-at-home motherhood, she started rebranding herself even before she had the business really up and running. Now when people asked her that loaded question that dogs almost every stay-at-home mom, "What do you do?" she'd reply, "I'm a photographer." Meanwhile, she geared up to make it a reality. Though she sometimes felt like a fraud saying it at first, hearing how the words sounded coming out of her mouth gave her something to be proud of and helped her regain her confidence. Mostly, she felt she was setting a great example for her daughter by showing her the importance of being independent, working hard, and being able to support oneself, with or without a husband. Erin found it extremely satisfying to have back her role as a career woman, and extra gratifying that it was in a different and better way than she'd expected it could be.

COMEBACK QUOTE

"I wish I had believed in myself and my skill, and my ability to make photography a thriving career much earlier, when I had the time to delve into studying it more intensely. It was much more difficult learning and perfecting the craft on limited time, and at the same time that I had to set up the nonartistic part of the business, like billing and marketing."

—Erin, photographer, mother of two

Find Seed Money

Starting a business often means coming up with seed money. Think about what tools and technology you'll need to start your business. Erin, for example, needed to invest in new equipment. Do you need a new computer? A scanner? Extra monitors? A new phone line? Business cards? Count on everything costing more than you think it will.

If you have money earned from your career pre-children, go ahead and invest in yourself if you can afford to. I don't suggest that everyone clean out her 401(k) on a whim, but if you have savings and it won't hurt your long-term retirement goal, I'm in favor of your using that money to launch something new that you believe in. I always prefer self-funding, if it's possible. If you are willing to take out a loan, your local or community bank will have information about small business loans. I am not a fan of taking money from friends and family, and I don't advise offering an ownership stake in your start-up business. We all have those relatives who have an opinion, whether you ask for it or not. Do you want that to be a part of your professional life going forward? This kind of arrangement can become further complicated when you are running your own multimillion-dollar enterprise someday! Start small, dream big, right? But start-up costs for any business, at home or otherwise, are going to be a reality.

Get Started on a Shoestring

Start-up costs can be large, but the good news is that with a little creativity you can get around some of the bigger expenses. Be cautious about having people do work up front on things like your website or design for a piece of the pie on the back end once you're up and running. It's easy to pay out 10 percent of your business to someone when you are making only ten thousand dollars a year, but if you strike it big (which you will), and your revenues start to be in the millions, handing over that 10 percent year after year to the kid who made your website will sting. Pay for things when you can. Decide what you can afford to spend and what's most critical to spend it on. Hit up successful friends for legal or marketing help and insight, and barter for services where possible.

Building your online platform can be expensive, but you can get one up and running before you have the money to pay a web developer. At the very least start a Facebook page. Then, when you can afford a website, have someone build one for you. Also, if you have an idea for a business name, secure it with GoDaddy, a web hosting service, so that if you are successful, you own the website. It's not that expensive to buy a dot-com name. I can't tell you how many people name and trademark their business, only to discover afterward that they can't buy the URL because someone is holding it hostage for thousands of dollars. Once you decide on a potential name for your business, do a domain search and buy it right away, before someone out there sees what you're searching, buys it out from under you, then demands a high price to sell it back. (Yes, the technology exists to let people do this.) You can set up corresponding Twitter, Instagram, Pinterest, and Facebook pages for free. And business cards can be made inexpensively through sites like Moo.com or VistaPrint.com.

Research, research, and research so whatever you buy gets you the most bang for your buck and the greatest ability to generate revenue. And find new ways to get what you need. For example: for every holiday, your anniversary, and your birthday, tell your husband and relatives you'd like a web design package or a desk built in the corner of the basement. Erin's equipment was expensive, so Christmas, birthday, and anniversary meant one good lens.

Take Appropriate Precautions

Be sure you don't cut any corners on legal or accounting issues. It's not a bad idea to form a Limited Liability Company (LLC) or S-Corp for tax and legal purposes. And get bank accounts and credit cards for the business so you keep church and state separate.

Depending on what sort of business you're in, you might look into insurance. For example, if you're like Erin and other photographers shooting weddings, you want to be protected from an angry bride if something goes terribly wrong and the photos of the big day are somehow destroyed.

Use Time Well

Because of their erratic schedules and hours, many moms won't be able to take classes once they decide to enter a new field or jump into their old one after several years away. They'll have to teach themselves. Erin wished she'd spent more time studying the technical aspects of photography and really cramming while her kids were babies. Looking back, she said if she had used the time while the children slept to stay on top of her interests, she could have better kept up on the shift from film to digital photography and not had to cram when she really wanted to dive right in. When she finally went pro and the work started pouring in, she had to learn a lot more on the job than she would have if she'd just studied the entire time she was home with the kids. By the time she really started trying to catch up, Erin was only able to study or take classes late at night online. There weren't a lot of in-person courses available at that hour so she taught herself what she could. Fortunately, one of the benefits of being a stay-at-home mom, and coming back to work before there was any pressing need, was that she wasn't tied to any deadline to find and build a passion into a new career.

Don't Be Rigid

Alita Guillen made a conscious decision to go into business for herself so that she could build a career around her life rather than the reverse. When she started thinking about ways to launch a start-up, her first decision was not to put all her eggs in one basket. Instead, she was willing to try everything and see what stuck. She ultimately launched

Guillen Media. The company was a success, but she found it isolating, and struggled with self-motivation. Eventually she launched a completely different business: Gadgit Girlz, a consumer goods company that she formed with a partner. She hadn't considered working with a partner for the first company because she thought it would drag her down, but in the end she loved having one. Collaboration proved to generate more creative and successful ideas, and having a partner kept her accountable to make sure things got done. Plus, she felt less vulnerable because she was only responsible for half of the cash outlay for the start-up, minimizing her risk.

Be Careful with Partnerships

Opposites attract. Alita and her partner, Celeste, formed a successful partnership because they complemented each other by each bringing something totally different to the table. That's the ticket to a great collaboration. If one person is great with numbers and one is great with marketing, that's a good match. But though your skill sets should be different, make sure you share the same business philosophy. Make it legal. Even if you're going into business with your very best friend, hire a lawyer to put together a legal agreement outlining the terms of your professional partnership. As Alita said, when it comes to money, friendship and a handshake won't do. Alita and Celeste got everything in writing, making sure they were equals in every way, but also outlined what would happen if the partnership dissolved or in the event that one of them wanted to walk away from the partnership.

Prepare for Surprising Challenges

Entrepreneurship doesn't always look the way you think it will, as Alita's story shows.

- Alita missed the identity that came with working for a big-brand company.

- It's not glamorous. Alita was the IT department, accounts receivable, filing person, and chief coffeemaker.

- She had to make it rain. If she didn't generate work, there was no money coming in. She would spend a little time each day prepping and scheduling tasks for the coming days, and on Sundays she would take twenty minutes to plan out her calls for the week to drum up new business.

- Time management seemed like it would have been the easiest part of the job since she was making her own hours, but working from home made it more difficult. There were a lot of interruptions. The kids, if you can believe it, expected to be fed, and driven to soccer and school, which meant that even if she was on a roll she couldn't just work until she was ready to stop. The solution is to outsource wherever possible so that you can concentrate as much as you can either on your work or the kids. If the kids aren't in school yet, find quality, reputable day care, or, if you can afford it, hire a nanny, even if it's only part time. Get a housecleaner, too, if you can afford it. And Crock-Pots are every working woman's friend.

- In order to avoid distractions like the pile of laundry beckoning to be washed, Alita often worked away from her home office. Some days Starbucks was her headquarters, especially if she had a lot of work to do on the computer, and she and Celeste often took walks together during their meetings.

- Alita didn't expect that she'd have to hide the kids from clients, but she became very good at it. She had to do it quite often, in fact, because she lived on the West Coast and frequently took calls from the East Coast, which was three hours ahead. It often happened that these calls had to take place while her children were getting ready for school. If she needed to pretend she was in an office and not at home (to improve her credibility and professional persona), she hopped in the car in the driveway to take a call. Her advice: don't ever give the client the illusion your attention is split between the kids and the gig. You want the person on the other end of the phone to picture you sitting in a big office, surrounded by help, running the show, not the real-life yoga-pants-wearing you with your hair in a ponytail.

Enjoy the Payoff

What Alita loves most about working for herself is that the harder she works, the greater the payoff. She makes sure she enjoys every minute of it and loves controlling her hours and her workload. But she acknowledges, it's not for everyone. It's hard work going it alone.

You can design your comeback in whichever way works best for you and your family. Whether you choose a straightforward reentry into your old career or something else, whether you start with full-time work, part-time work, or an internship, or you start a company of your own—the options are varied. Just leave yourself room to adjust as needed, and know the pros and cons of your choices. Nothing is easy, but every option has benefits. Heed the advice of the smart women you just met as you blaze your trail, wherever it might lead you. Now get out there and take action.

7

——

The Interview

S o you've done your homework, figured out your timing, assessed your career, identified your next steps, and now you have an interview. Don't fear the interview—celebrate it! Half the battle to your comeback is getting someone to notice you, and if you've got an interview, you did just that. Congrats!

You managed to impress someone enough to hire you years ago when you started your first career; you can do it again. Don't think of your interviewer as an adversary. His or her goal isn't to set you up or make you feel stupid; it's to get to know you and your skill set, and see if you and the company are a good fit. And that goes both ways. This is your chance to evaluate the company and management, too. Don't worry about the long-term stakes; just try to focus on getting the most information possible and making the best impression you can within the short amount of time available to you.

Now, how do you do that?

Do your research. Smart job hunters do their mom homework *before* applying for and accepting a job in order to find the best fit and limit unhappy surprises.

Internet search. Vet a company for family-friendliness by searching for information in the public sphere. Many company websites include HR information, magazines such as *Working Mother* and *Forbes* publish employee satisfaction rankings, and the first-person reviews on the website Glassdoor can give you the real skinny about what it's like to work at a particular company.

Interview moms. Odds are good you picked your stroller or summer camp after hearing rave reviews from a fellow mom. Use that same mom-tested wisdom to assess employers. LinkedIn and Facebook are the perfect research tools, letting you easily identify who in your network has a connection who can share the inside track.

Compare and contrast. Can't find information on a company? Make an educated guess by looking for information on similar employers or about the industry in general. Again, LinkedIn is a useful resource: find connections in roles to the one you're applying for and interview them to see if their experience makes the company sound fair and appealing.

Look the Part

Invest in two new interview outfits. Why two? Because this will be like a date; if the interviewer wants to see you again (or have her colleagues meet you), you'll get another call, and you won't want to wear the same thing twice. Research your industry to figure out how conservatively or casually you should dress, though even if you're interviewing with a tiny shop founded by hipsters, your safest bet is to dress slightly more formally than the place might demand. You can always relax and show your true colors once you're hired (unless you're in banking, which really seems to allow only two: black and navy).

Do whatever it takes to make you feel your best. Self-conscious about your teeth? Get them whitened. Not loving the gray streaks? Hit the salon. Borrow the right accessories for a polished look if money is an issue. A new bag, pair of earrings, or power heels can make an outfit, and make you feel like a million bucks. But do all of this for yourself, not for the interviewer. What's most important is that you go into that interview projecting confidence and a can-do spirit. If you know you're awesome and could do the job better than anyone else, you'll have an easier time persuading others to think so, too.

Take the advice I've lived by since the first time I heard it: When you walk into a room, any room, offer a smile right away. Nothing sets the tone better. Hold your head up and your shoulders back, offer a firm handshake (practice with your husband or a friend if you need to figure out the appropriate grip), and let your smile banish any hint of stress or fear. Your goal is to convey the utmost confidence and professionalism. Don't fidget or look around the room, and put your phone away and out of sight. Maintain good eye contact.

Body Language

Body language is key when you sit down for an interview. In fact, body language is a huge part of what I do as a news anchor. I have to present an air of authority, confidence, and openness to a television audience. Here are some of my tricks.

Don't:

- cross your arms over your chest

- look down at the floor

- slouch or lean too far back in your chair

- tilt your head either left or right when listening

Do:

- sit up straight

- cross your legs at the knee or ankle

- grip your crossed knee for stability to calm your nerves

- rotate your shoulders back and down

- place one hand on top of the other in your lap

- keep your chin up (just like you did in school pictures)

- breathe slowly in and out through your nose

Sound the Part

Do your homework before you walk through the door. Buy the company's product or try to take advantage of their service so you can speak as a knowledgeable consumer. Be familiar with their history and their recent or noteworthy accomplishments. Take opportunities to let your interviewer know that you've been following the company and can speak intelligently about their product, service, growth, even awards received. Whenever possible, draw connections between your experience and their needs, or express how you could help further their goals and support their team. Don't make them have to figure out for themselves where you'd fit in—you want to do as much thinking as possible for your future employer. Make it easy for people to see you in the role you want. Practice interviewing with friends and especially old colleagues, who may be better able to prepare you for the gamut of questions someone might ask and help you fine-tune your answers. You want to be able to speak with so much poise and confidence that when you leave, the people who interviewed you will be holding you up as the gold standard against which they compare everyone else who applies for the position.

Take it from a news reporter: ask questions, and then *listen*. I can't tell you how many jobs I landed where the person conducting the interview talked twice as much as I did. They are giving you valuable information, and in their mind, your ability to listen shows confidence, intellect, and a willingness to learn. Let them do the talking.

What to Say/What Not to Say

There is no getting around the question you will almost certainly be asked: "Why are you interested in coming back to work?" This is one of the most important things you will need to prepare for during the interview process. Have your response ready and rehearsed. Don't say "Because we need the money." Instead have a power line ready to go that you have rehearsed with your friends and/or spouse, such as "I'm ready for a new challenge and this job will give me that and more." Or "I miss being part of the xxx industry. I didn't realize how much until I wasn't an active participant on a day-to-day basis."

Don't Talk Mom

Working moms are understandably interested in getting the information they need to determine if a company will allow them to successfully balance work and family. But bringing up your baby or kids in a job interview can send the wrong message. Don't try to hide the fact that you have children, but don't bring it up, either. If your interviewer mentions his or her children, then maybe you can find rapport by mentioning that you have kids as well, but it should be an aside. You want to keep the interview focused on you and your skills because, as Katie Fogarty said, prospective employers can become concerned that you're not going to focus 100 percent on the job. They are hiring you, not you and Junior.

Which is not to say you shouldn't consider your kids when deciding which companies you want to pursue. Some recruiters and coaches interviewed for this book said it's OK to ask about hours and flexibility. Most said you're better off knowing in advance that you have to stay until midnight on Tuesday twice a month than not. But don't frame the question as a working mom's question. Rather, ask, "How would you describe the culture of your company?" "Is your busy period cyclical or constant?" If you hear words or phrases like *intense* and *tough*, and *weekend warrior*, or anecdotes that always seem to start with the team still in the office eating takeout at 10 p.m., it could be a warning that it won't be a family-friendly environment. That said, know your audience. If you're interviewing with a financial services firm requiring an eighty-hour workweek, you're probably not going to get any flextime.

Counter Shortcomings with Strengths

Tracey had always worked in the restaurant business. As a waitress, she had been trained the old-school way to focus on customers, offer impeccable service, and know how to perform under pressure. By the time she decided to go back to work, however, the industry had completely changed. In particular, it had been automated, and Tracey had no experience with the new technology. She knew she could learn it all, but none of the big restaurant chains were willing to take a chance on her.

Tracey was frustrated. The staff at all of these restaurants was young. They may have been sharp on systems that were used for point of sale, placing orders, examining eating trends, and communicating with the kitchen, but she had eaten at these establishments and knew their waitstaff was completely untrained in all the important customer service skills Tracey had—skills that may not benefit management or the back of the house so much but that do create satisfied, loyal, repeat customers. After a few interviews and three missed job opportunities, she realized she had to change her approach.

Tracey stepped back, took a short break from her job search, and spent that time analyzing what had gone wrong in all three missed gigs. She reviewed what had been said to her in each interview and the explanation she'd received for not landing each job. Knowing her shortcomings, she set out to highlight her strengths. And she changed her targets.

Tracey approached a non–chain restaurant opening up in her area—not quite a tiny mom-and-pop operation, but a family business. The owners already had one restaurant in town and were opening a second. Before the issue of technology came up, Tracey put it out there herself. She said very clearly, "I don't know how to work the computer you have, but I'll learn in a week, I promise. In addition, I will train your entire staff. I can do that, that's what I'm good at." She chose not to try to hide her lack of technology know-how, but instead trumped it with something even better.

Armed with a preemptive strike and the smarts to learn what to say from her previous interviews, Tracey impressed the owner of the restaurant. She thought Tracey's plan was brilliant, and was thrilled to have an older employee she could rely on to teach the customer service skills the younger generation had not yet learned. Five years in, the owner and Tracey are not only friends, but the owner also has said frequently that hiring Tracey was the best decision she had ever made.

Tracey's strategy was similar to a trick we use in news meetings: if you come to the meeting armed with an idea, you won't get stuck on a story you don't want to do. You've done the thinking and planning for the assignment editor, saving him or her the task of having to figure something out. Don't be a sitting duck, ashamed of what you don't know. Admit it and tell an employer what you *do* know.

> ## TAKE EACH NEGATIVE AND MAKE IT A POSITIVE
>
> - So you don't know the computer system. What do you know that a new employee doesn't? Face-to-face skills? Backroom management? Experience counts, and you have it.
> - What can you offer that won't be available without you?
> - What's the one big strength you have that nobody else has?

The Final Question

At the end of almost every interview, you'll usually be asked whether you have any questions. The answer should always be yes. Always keep one question on hold for this very moment. It makes you look good, like you're really eager to learn more and don't want the conversation to end. In the mind of an interviewer, someone who doesn't have any questions probably isn't thinking hard enough.

Some good questions for you to ask, either throughout your interview or for your final question, could be:

- How is the management team organized?

- Who are the hiring managers?

- What's the leadership like?

- What's the potential for growth at the company? Do you promote from within?

- What other responsibilities would I be expected to assume, besides the ones you've already explained?

Think Small

As Tracey figured out, you might have more of a shot at effecting change and overcoming your shortcomings if you bypass the biggest players in the game and target smaller companies. A smaller company might be more willing to teach you the ropes. Consider where you could offer a special talent they might be short on. During the interview, offer to do something in addition to the job you're being brought in to do, like start a committee, do some training, or develop a strategy for new hires with little job experience. That's tricky, of course—you don't want to overload yourself. But it might be a worthwhile strategy, at least for the short term, so you can get that first job experience and beef up your résumé.

You don't have to reserve those good ideas for small companies, of course. It's just that big companies might move slowly and be less open to that sort of flexibility and outside-the-box thinking. If you land a job in a bigger company, you might be better able to sell that idea once inside. It will show you have initiative and surely help you move up in the ranks faster.

Be Resilient

Renate was organized and on the ball, and more than ready for her big interview at a retail store the following day. She'd arranged for child care for her three children, printed her résumé, and had her clothing out and ready for the morning. When she awoke to an ice storm (nearly unheard of in Dallas), she scrambled. She called the store to confirm that she was indeed on her way and to make sure her potential future employer would be, too. She left with plenty of weather-worked-in time to spare. Still, traffic was a disaster as everyone crawled along the icy streets, and she arrived twenty minutes late. Nerves already rattled, she faced a nasty, dismissive store manager who refused to even interview her because of her tardiness. Worse, the manager tipped off Renate's current employer that she was out looking for another job. Renate didn't get the job, but she was fueled by that disaster of an interview and the manager's extreme rudeness. She built up her courage for the next interview and went in there like she didn't care if she landed the job or not. Her attitude was brilliant—much improved over the previous experience. She nailed the interview and got the job. Her big takeaway: don't sweat the jobs you don't get. Consider those interviews practice runs. Each one will help you build your skills and confidence and teach you something you can use the next time.

Follow Up

Realize that no employer is going to work as fast as you'd like them to work. I know people who have spent six to nine months interviewing with an interested company, conducting repeated meetings and calls and experiencing long stretches of radio silence before finally learning they'd landed a gig.

There are a few things you can do while playing the waiting game.

Mailing a handwritten thank-you note is an opportunity to have the last word at your interview. When I receive a handwritten note these days, it's a rare occurrence. I remember who sent it and appreciate the effort. Stand out this way. Use it to remind potential employers of the most important things you said while in the office, or to bring up a funny moment or establish more rapport. And then, be patient. With any luck you'll get a second interview, or maybe even a job offer. You might also get a pass. Don't let it get you down. Instead, treat it as a learning experience.

- If you've missed a gig, like Tracey did, make a list of the five things that went wrong and then figure out how you're going to do better next time.

- Don't hesitate to call the headhunter or person who interviewed you and find out where you came up short or why you didn't get the job. If you're given a concrete reason why you weren't as qualified as someone else, do what you can to shore up that weakness. Sometimes, though, you'll find out that you didn't get the job for a reason that is completely out of your control. Take heart that you did your very best, and move on. And if you can, make clear that you enjoyed the interview very much and that you hope you'll be remembered the next time there's an opening at the company. In fact, I had an informational interview at Fox three years before a job opportunity presented itself, and that same executive remembered me when I walked into his office in November of 2006.

- Most important: nothing is a job until you have an offer. Be diligent about not ending your search the first time someone says, "We'd love to have you on board." Corporate head counts, job shuffles, and a number of other factors unrelated to you or your abilities could affect whether you actually get the job. Stay calm. Be patient. Keep your eyes open for other opportunities until the paperwork is signed.

The big thing to realize is that with any interview, you want to be yourself. The best kind of interviews are the ones that don't actually feel like interviews, just conversations between two people with similar interests. Get through those initial few seconds, and once you start connecting with your interviewer, you'll probably start to relax and, if all goes really well, you might even start to enjoy yourself. No need to worry about negotiating your salary or work/life balance now. If you make it clear that you are the best person for this job, you will have more leverage for negotiating an arrangement that helps you get the work/life balance you want.

8

Get What You Want—Ten Tips for Negotiating a Killer Deal

So you got the interview and landed a job offer. Congrats! But don't relax yet. You'll want to be on your toes about negotiating a deal that will be the best possible arrangement for you and your family.

Many women dread negotiations—I know I do, which is why I'm thankful for my agent and wish everyone could have one. Most television news reporters, anchors, and even producers do. The job of the agent is to negotiate on my behalf and that of my colleagues so that we can keep our relationship with our company somewhat clean and separate, leaving us to focus on being creative, hardworking journalists and performers. My agent, Laurie Jacoby, has been with me from my days in San Francisco. She works with a team of people at Napoli Management in Los Angeles whose sole focus is getting their clients the right job, in the right city, under the right circumstances. In addition, Laurie also raised two amazing children in her thirty years as a talent agent. When I started thinking about who could best advise a working mom on how to negotiate a favorable job agreement, my first stop was Laurie.

According to Laurie, there are several things that women going back into the workforce, whatever their job is, need to remember as they try to negotiate the best possible deal.

1. Take the "I can't do this" out of your head. Here's why: Your kids are constantly trying to get you to negotiate. Can we have an ice cream on the way home? Your answer: "Yes, but that means no ice cream after dinner." Negotiation complete. You also negotiate with your spouse about everything from where you're going out for dinner to when and if you're heading to visit the relatives. It's endless. It's life. And you navigate both the calm waters and the rough seas. I promise you this is something you can do.

2. Always be optimistic. This cliché holds true: where there is a will there is a way. If the two parties want to come together, they will. You've done a darn good job in the interview process and the company is serious about trying to hire you or you wouldn't be in this position. An offer likely won't be rescinded if you ask for more money than was originally offered *and can make a case for it*. There's generally wiggle room in a corporate offer, especially for higher-ranking positions.

3. You will likely be asked how much you were earning in your last position. Don't discuss your previous salary if it isn't relevant. If you held your last position ten or twenty years ago, the answer isn't relevant, and you can say so. Just say politely that the position and salary would not be applicable today.

4. Employers will sometimes ask you, "What salary would you want?" Don't ever be the first one to lay a number on the table. Consider, for example, that you would be more than happy to earn $50,000 for the position. If you throw that figure out it's very possible that the company was thinking they would offer $62,000, and now this interviewer wants to give herself a high five because she knows she can close the deal and make her bosses happy that she saved them $12,000. Let the employer start the bidding. When a potential employer asks Laurie the salary question regarding one of her clients, she often says, "A million-five!" as a joke. Assuming your salary wouldn't be anywhere near that, the response you'd get is probably the same one she gets: there is a beat, and then a laugh. Every time. It never fails. We'd all want a million-five or ten million or one hundred million! It's a great way to deflect the question and put it back on them. If the interviewer laughs and then says, "Seriously, what type of salary are you looking for?" your response should be "I'm just looking for a fair offer that is commensurate with the work I'll be doing. I'm just excited for this new opportunity."

5. Do enough research to know what's coming and how to make a case for more. Sometimes you'll just be told in no uncertain terms, "This is the salary and here are the benefits." The company doesn't necessarily expect you to question it. But there is often room for negotiation, and you will not know that unless you try. So if you get an offer, be ready to counter with your proposal—higher salary, shorter hours, one day of work from home, whatever it is that you're looking for. They may tell you they have four other candidates. Could be true. But you are their first choice or you wouldn't be getting the offer. So be in the driver's seat.

6. If negotiating for a higher salary, know what you have to have and what you want, and then ask for something a little higher. You want the employer to be able to come back to you with a lower offer that hits your sweet spot. Of course, if you have drawn a line in the sand and are willing to walk away if you can't get the salary you want, be honest about that. Tell them what you need to make an agreement, but also explain why you deserve it.

It's not the employer's problem if you need more money to pay for the cost of child care, even if you're a single mother. However, assess the situation. Remember Dolores, the Harvard-educated attorney who had to start her comeback as a temp at a financial services firm? When she found herself negotiating one job while still holding on to another, she was able to negotiate properly and aggressively. That's not to say it was easy for her to ask. The package was already generous and she was afraid she'd put her new employer off. But she had a few key pieces of information. She knew that the only time to get the money she needed would be upon entry; raises didn't happen in any dramatic fashion at that company. She knew the head of HR was a mother and thought she might get a sympathetic ear. Finally, she also knew she was the best person for the job and that the company would not find someone with her skill set to replace her if she walked away from the offer.

She felt certain the offer wouldn't be rescinded, so asking for more was OK. So she made an appointment with HR and explained that she was the sole breadwinner and she couldn't make ends meet if she didn't get a higher salary that allowed her to cover the costs of child care, especially when the job would require her to put in a million hours. She hoped they could work out an arrangement in which she would receive less in possible bonuses and more in up-front pay. She got what she asked for. She just had to be brave enough to ask for it.

Once Dolores got the salary she wanted, she never mentioned her family situation at work again. When her kids were with their father, she worked longer hours to compensate for the days she had to make it home for dinner. She never showed up to work complaining about how challenging it was to get the kids off to school. She never mentioned that she was in the middle of a very stressful divorce, going to depositions. She didn't say a word about any of that. She just went to work, to work. In the end, she got exactly what she needed to provide for her children, and relaunch a stellar career. Dolores is an inspiration to every working mom out there. That said, choose your battles carefully. Your employer doesn't care that you have kids who need braces, or that college costs so much, and yes, they have noticed that the cost of groceries has gone up. My agent once had a client who wanted her to explain to a manager that he needed a higher salary because his water bill had increased and he needed to fill his pool. Sorry, but nobody is going to be sympathetic to something like that. Remember, everyone has a reason why they need or want more money, but yours should relate to your skills, your seasoning, and your attention to detail. Your negotiating power will depend on how valuable and distinctive you are.

7. Don't sell yourself short. Talk about your accomplishments. Talk about your expertise. Don't be afraid to say what you've done and how you did it. Then explain why that should be properly compensated. Make your case—this is your chance to sell yourself. This should not be a daunting task. You are worth every penny a company will pay you. Lack of confidence makes too many women stumble during negotiations and take what they can get, especially moms who have been out of the workforce for a while.

8. Don't be unreasonable. If you've done your homework and know the position generally pays in the $60,000 to $80,000 range, don't ask for $120,000 and expect anyone to take you seriously. You will seem arrogant.

9. Think about benefits besides money that might satisfy you in your negotiation. More vacation time? Flexible hours?

Tickets to a yearly conference? Those things are currency. Asking for a continuing education stipend or tuition for a course might be worth negotiating if you want to grow in your career, and you could bring your new knowledge back to the company.

Carey was grateful to have found a job at all, especially considering the state of the economy when she started looking. She landed a teaching position at a local community college. It had been a smooth transition. She had a great boss, wonderful co-workers who also had chosen the field because it fit their family's lifestyle, and no trouble with office politics. But several months in she was still reeling from the amount she was paid for her work—less than $50,000, an enormous cut from her previous job. Though she could have worked more, she made herself stick to her contracted thirty-five hours per week. After a year or so, she started to look for work outside of her small town, knowing she could make a higher salary doing the same job on a larger campus in a larger city. But when she really looked at her cost of living, she quickly realized she was already well ahead of the game. Plus, she had summers off, which reduced her child-care costs dramatically. So in the end, the entirety of her job and how well it suited her life—the hours, the negligible commute, the cost of living, the flexibility, the low stress, the likable co-workers—made up for the low income, and even made her realize that for where she lived, it wasn't that low.

10. If you are offered a position, you do not need to respond with a counteroffer immediately. Thank the hiring agent for the offer, agree that you understand what you're being offered, and say that you need a day or the weekend to think about it. That gives you time to form your response. When it's all said and done you may get everything, something, or nothing more than the original offer. But the important thing to remember is that you gave it a shot.

You Are a Valuable Resource

Sharon O'Connor, EdD psychologist, is both a mom and a professional. Instead of letting a corporation or precedent determine how she'd balance her time, she took matters into her own hands. She partnered with two other women, who were also moms, to form DKS Consulting Group—a career development and executive coaching firm. They decided to build a business that put family first, and so created an environment that allowed for flexibility. If one was being pulled away for a mom issue, another could step in and help a client. They took a team approach. Her advice for working moms negotiating their first job back or an upgrade in their existing job: you are a valuable resource and deserve to be paid as such, even if you're working part time or a flex schedule.

A lawyer who was one of Sharon's clients had a schedule that required her to work four days a week (she was not going in on Wednesdays), and Saturdays and Sundays. Still, she didn't feel that she could ask for the money she was worth, even though she was billing more hours than her male colleagues. DKS helped her understand that just because she was taking Wednesday off she was still billing more hours than her peers who were working full time. This empowered her to ask for more money and get it.

For many women, negotiating is the most difficult aspect of the job hunt. And there is a double standard: women aren't expected to negotiate. I say: Do not let that double standard stop you. Ask for what you're worth. You want to find the companies that encourage equality. Be strong and bold, and let's start changing the working world's expectations not just toward moms, but also toward all women.

Part III

———

Living Your

Comeback

9

—

Common Challenges, and How Moms
Overcome Them

Once you start working again, you may discover that things have changed even more than you realized since you last earned a paycheck. Or you might discover, for better or for worse, that everything is still pretty much how you remembered it. You might run into a few surprises. Some will be wonderful; some might be unpleasant. How you deal with those unpleasant ones will determine the success of your comeback. None of the women you're about to meet found the road to theirs to be as smooth as they might have hoped, but they sure didn't let that stop them. If you ever find yourself in similar situations, your experience as a mom will be in your favor. After all, nothing is better at teaching you how to juggle, improvise, adapt, and make things happen than motherhood.

When You're Met with Resentment

Katharine thought she had negotiated the perfect job. A skilled social worker for a school, she had been allowed to create a part-time position for herself after taking a short maternity leave. The educators in the building, however, weren't entitled to that same opportunity. They had to take leave and work full time upon return. The result? Resentment and even outright hostility. At first it was subtle. When Katharine asked questions, she'd get snarky answers like, "Well, we learned that new computer change during your days off," or, "Yes, there have been some philosophical changes made while you were out." Eventually, the resentment exploded into all-out arguments. Katharine felt blindsided and attacked.

To solve her problem, she tapped her skills and went into social worker mode. She decided to tackle the issue head-on and ask some tough questions, even though the answers might be hard to hear. She approached the colleagues with whom she was having the most friction and asked, "What's at the heart of your frustration?"

These were some of their answers:

• We're tired.

• We have to pick up the slack for you.

• We thought you were part of the team, the big picture, but you come in a couple of days, do your job, and go home with no help or backup for the institution in general.

• We're tired of covering for you and wasting our time filling in for you while you're away.

At first, she was hurt. Then Katharine took a step back and put herself in her colleagues' shoes. How would she feel if she had to pick up the slack for others? After all, everyone was busy, not just Katharine. The other women at work also had to go home and raise kids and run errands. Katharine hadn't ever pondered their perspective.

Next, she asked the group for a list of very specific things she could do to alleviate the resentment:

- What specifically can I do to support you?

- What can I do to demonstrate that I value our working relationship?

It took a lot of work, but she caught up. She started to be very aware that when she was away during a crisis, her colleagues were jumping in on their own to solve the problem. She had thought it was enough to say that she was available by phone and e-mail on her days off if the team needed her, but now she made it clear that not only was she to be contacted in the event of a crisis, she also would be the one who would deal with it. She realized it was her professional responsibility to be on call all of the time, even when she was "off."

If you've negotiated for something most people at your company don't have, be sensitive to that. Make an extra effort to connect with team members, and be aware that part time might look different from what you thought. It might just mean more flexibility, not necessarily fewer hours. But consider this: in today's corporate environment, few people are working forty hours a week, so it's slightly naïve to think part time equals a twenty-hour week.

On the flipside, if you're working full time and you have a colleague who has more flexibility than you, try to curb your resentment. How can you work together to make the situation between you more equitable without insulting or directly challenging that colleague? If you are feeling like the situation is still unfair, then set up a meeting with your boss to propose a system that works for you. Again, bosses don't want to have to sit and think about your problems. Always come in with a proposed solution. The easier you can make their lives, the better, and you never want to be labeled a "complainer" so be careful how you characterize the struggles you are having.

When You Don't Fit In

Roberta worked in the fast-paced world of TV news, a career she loved. The days were long—sometimes twelve hours—and when news broke, she had to drop everything and get into the office. Her husband worked in the same business, and once they had children, they realized that they couldn't both work jobs that required such long, unpredictable hours. Staying home full time wasn't an option, so Roberta took a step back and tried to assess what sort of job would work for her and her family. She decided to get a teaching degree, take a teaching job, and while doing that earn a graduate degree to become a librarian, something she'd always wanted to do. She got lucky, and after she graduated she landed a dream job as a school librarian—not only did she run the library, but the school had a media program, so she ran the TV studio there as well. She took a substantial pay cut, but felt the lower pay was fair because she had summers off and a schedule that allowed her to be home with the kids before 4 p.m.

Roberta was by far the oldest person at her school and, surprisingly, the only one with kids at home. When she first started, she felt torn and pressured. Her colleagues were young and they wanted to go out on Friday nights with fellow teachers and hit happy hour. She wanted to go home and see her small children. Her priorities weren't aligned with everyone else's. Not only did this divergence prevent her from forming any friendships, it meant at work she was constantly on the outs, if only because nobody had a chance to get to know her.

Roberta made a choice. Once a month she would make a sacrifice at home and join her co-workers for a drink after work. She arranged for her parents to watch her kids and she made an effort to go and get to know her fellow teachers. The result was transformative. "I found that after I started doing that, more people would stop in the library to see me or people would want to collaborate more with me because they had gotten to know me a little better." That small effort proved valuable in another way as well, one that paid off at home. "I love my job," says Roberta. "And because I loved my job when my kids were little, I always came home happy. So to be happy in your job, to be happy at work all day, you come home happy, and I think it just makes for a happier home life. It really does."

When You're the Oldest One in the Room

Remember Karyn from chapter 6, who turned a volunteer position into a full-time paid job? She worked in a young office at a young person's level. The executives, however, like her, were not born in the eighties, but were earning much higher incomes and therefore could afford nannies. Karyn had to call on her mother and sometimes neighbors to help with child care. It made her self-conscious. She also started to notice that she was being excluded from a lot of social events because she was the oldie at work. She knew that socializing was part of the game, and that deals were often struck after hours, but she had zero time to participate in it.

On the other hand, Karyn discovered that her age gave her an edge over her young, fresh-out-of-school colleagues. Every so often, her bosses would ask her to attend a meeting even though she was junior on the staff. They wanted her there because they knew she carried herself well and would be taken seriously by older clients, many of whom were the heads of major firms.

In addition, her superiors recognized that she had something no one else had: contacts from the military—not the type that could have landed her a job, but ones that proved helpful in her current one. She could call the Pentagon, and she could help clients get in touch with appropriate parties that her peers could not.

COMEBACK QUOTE

"Corporate America had changed and I definitely felt older [but] now I [had] some time and experience under my belt so I think I had a different perspective, and in some ways I was more confident because of [my] age."

—Lori, TV producer, two children

Karyn's age was a double-edged sword, but she used her life experience and her people skills to her benefit. Perhaps because she was older, wiser, and more mature, she knew how to navigate the pitfalls of her situation. Take a page from her book by following her strategies:

• Don't be shy about showing your value.

• Find a niche, something that you are good at.

- Be a workhorse while at work.

- Make yourself invaluable and irreplaceable.

- Make it impossible for a company or client to ignore you.

The commute and child care eventually became untenable, but Karyn proved herself so much to the company that her supervisors agreed to let her work as a full-time contractor. She was able to move back upstate and work from home. She was taken off the payroll and so lost all of her benefits like health insurance and a 401(k), but now she was able to drop off and pick up her children herself. She was vulnerable without health insurance (this was before the Affordable Care Act) but within months, she parlayed the contract work into a great local gig with benefits.

Lori, too, had to overcome the age barrier. She was an anomaly at the TV news network where she worked. She had two busy teenagers at home to shuttle around. She loved her job, but there was a lot of social activity after hours, and raising two children and working full time didn't allow for much of that. Since she couldn't go out with her colleagues during traditional happy hour, she found other ways to ingratiate herself and become a part of the "club." Here are some of her ideas:

- Find a different way to integrate—have coffee with colleagues during the day or grab lunch.

- Pick and choose—every casual after-hours drink is not crucial, but some events will be important. Figure out what those are and make it a point to attend. Otherwise, commit to making it to one out-of-office event a month.

- Make time for developing a network so you're thought of at promotion time.

- If there's an office gym, use it. Find unique ways to socialize and be a part of that scene.

- Take advantage of any networking programs offered at the company. Lori's company had what was called a 360 program, where you could meet people from different levels for a chat. She took advantage of it and at one meeting interacted with someone she never would have otherwise who later thought of her for a job within the company. If your boss is reluctant to give you time off during the day to attend such a program, put together a compelling case for why it would benefit your work or her department.

Whatever you do, don't go to work with your defenses up, assuming everyone will treat you like a relic. Even if your boss is younger than you, he or she might actually look up to you. Don't assume everyone who's your junior is a selfie-loving narcissist or incapable of writing anything but acronyms. Give everyone, no matter what their age, a chance—just like you hope they'll give you a chance. Get to know them and understand them. You might be pleasantly surprised by how you and your younger counterparts complement one another, and how learning more about the younger generations' interests and technology might help you in your work.

At the same time, don't adopt youth-speak. One bonus to being the oldest person in the room: you don't talk like the young techie generation. This gives you credibility with more senior staff and can help set you apart in a good way. Don't start speaking hipster just to keep up. Your experience will trump age.

Finally, don't scoff at menial tasks. Even if some jobs feel beneath you, demonstrate maturity by making clear you'll do whatever needs to get done. If you excel at "boring" tasks, you may be given more responsibility. You have to prove yourself more than the rest of the crowd. Stay determined and do every task well, no matter how menial. You'll show up those kids who get out of college and immediately think they can rule the world five minutes into a gig.

We all grapple with aging. It's inevitable. I feel old on some days, too. My advice? Get over it. You need to be strategic and find common ground with the younger generation in your industry and make this work. Celebrate your age and your experience—it has filled you with qualities that only come birthday after birthday.

When You Don't Get the Technology

Technology changes in a nanosecond these days. Right there, as you read that sentence—it changed. Your phone is old practically before you get it home. It's no surprise, then, that once you head back to work, especially if you've been out for a while, things will have changed.

I've met women who left the workforce before the BlackBerry made its mark, who walked away before e-mail became the way most people now communicate. Then they tried to come back and were overwhelmed by how many new systems there were to learn and how important social media had become. And coming back can be truly daunting for those who left before social media became part of the company toolbox and even the lowliest assistant had to keep a professional blog. Daunting, but not impossible. Many of the moms I spoke to struggled hard with the transition, but also managed to conquer the problem.

Katharine, the social worker, was used to walking down to someone's office to communicate, or picking up the phone to talk through a situation. She was accustomed to regular meetings where people actually sat in the same room. When she returned after raising kids, everything had changed. Most business was handled through e-mail, there were few meetings, and face-to-face interaction had been nearly eliminated. This posed a few problems for Katharine. E-mails gave her no way to gauge people's moods; she had to learn to read between the lines and figure out this new method of communication. She was used to handwritten comments on documents, but now everything was done electronically, and she found the programs onerous and not user-friendly. She felt completely alienated and missed the sense of teamwork she remembered from her old job.

How did she survive? She just dove right in and kept trying. The only way to survive such a trial by fire, according to Katharine, is to accept that you will make mistakes. Own them. Learn from them. Most important, do not be afraid to ask for help. Her secret: ask the youngest person there. I can actually vouch for that strategy. How do you think that I learned to use Twitter? When I realized I needed to figure it out, I asked someone much younger and way cooler than me to explain how to use it effectively. Katherine, like me, found her younger co-workers to be more receptive and better able to explain the advancements in technology since they were the first adopters. I imagine that an even better choice would be to find the youngest mom you can and ask her for help.

Nancy, the doctor we met in chapter 3 who ran into trouble when she let her credentials expire, faced a lot of prejudice and frustration when she started her fellowship. She had no trouble with the medical aspects of her job—it was the workflow and systems at her hospital that were causing her difficulty. Most people in her position were coming right off their residencies. They were younger than she was, and she had been out of work for so long that at times she didn't even know what questions to ask.

Looking back, Nancy wishes she'd asked to shadow someone initially rather than struggle on her own to understand the systems. A month would have been a game changer.

She also wishes she'd spoken up and asked for time to catch up. If she'd suggested starting as a shadow, she would have learned quicker, assimilated sooner, and frustrated her co-workers less.

If you've been out for a while, learn a few lessons from Nancy's experience.

- Speak up immediately and admit where you might initially need some help.

- Consider that you might not even know you'll need that help, so ask about how the landscape has changed since you've been gone—then find an ally who can offer some helpful guidance.

- Ask your supervisor if you could spend one week to one month shadowing another employee or learning the systems if you feel you'll need to.

- Don't reveal to everyone that you're a working mom returning after a gap, but carefully target the superior who might
  be able to help and ask him or her, before it's too late, the best
  way to bring you up to speed quickly.

If you are going back to a field like real estate where you know a
specific software program is being used, take online courses to get
familiar with it. They are the cheapest and easiest way to go. Even
community colleges and universities are teaching most courses online.
Most employers will expect you to come to the table with a working
knowledge of Word, PowerPoint, Excel, and basic office management
software. If you do not have it, then you need to acquire it either
through online course work, or through lynda.com or LinkedIn. You
don't need to physically go back to school to get caught up on your
tech. Hire a neighbor's college- or even high school–age kid to teach
you basic programs if you need to learn them.[20] Heck, ask *your* school-
age kids to teach you how to use apps and programs. Using tech is like
breathing to them.

Above all, don't be intimidated. You can learn this just like you
learned everything else. If you are far behind the curve on the tech
front, do a tiny something each day to improve upon it. It's all most
daunting in the early stages—it will get easier, and eventually you
won't feel so behind.

---

20. Interview with Carol Fishman Cohen, iRelaunch.

When You Feel Guilty

Karyn also struggled with the guilt she felt about not spending as much time with her kids as she used to. She was so determined to establish herself and get noticed that sometimes her days went from 7 a.m. to 7 p.m. She constantly had to explain to them that she didn't have a choice—she needed to make money. But they were too young to understand. They wanted her home.

Tanya was once a talent booker. She knew after leaving that field that at some point she'd return to work once her children were old enough. She figured out similarities between entertainment and publishing, exploited them on her résumé, and eventually ended up making the shift to publishing.

Once back, Tanya was the only worker in her office with kids, but unlike Karyn, she didn't struggle with guilt for being at work instead of at home. She quickly learned the kids were OK even though she was away. Her wisdom should ease the mind and heart of any mom worried that she is somehow letting her kids down by going to work.

Embrace the notion that it takes a village to raise a kid. Trust other people. "I thought before that if I couldn't be the helicopter-hovering mom and always have my arms halfway around them, protect them, and raise them just the way I wanted, that something bad would happen to them. But as I saw other people having positive influences on my daughters and teaching them things that maybe I wasn't as good at teaching them, or just interacting with them in ways that made them happy, I realized it's a good thing to have multiple people in their lives who are either role models or nurture them in ways different from me. That's a good thing, I believe. And so I stopped beating myself up about it."

Once the kids are old enough, involve them to a certain extent in what you do at work. Tanya said that took a big load off for her. She would have her older daughter sit down with her while she was working at home, and Tanya would talk through what she was doing. She said it made for a major shift—her daughter appreciated her efforts and said as much, too.

Remember that you are not alone. Almost all the other mothers in the workforce are in the same boat. If you work in an office where there aren't any mothers, you probably need to be a little extra communicative. For example, you might make sure everyone knows that you are 100 percent into your work and will do whatever you can to get things done while you're at the office, but that you have to leave at five because day care closes at six. That's a situation that is out of your control. Show everyone that you mean it—that you really are 100 percent invested while at work—and you will likely meet with much less grumbling when you have to bail in the middle of a crash project. Not everyone naturally understands what it's like to raise a child, so be proactive so that people know that you are doing your best.

COMEBACK QUOTE

"A mistake that I made was apologizing at work when I wasn't there, and apologizing to my kids when I wasn't with them. The guilt will eat away at you. You need to feel good about the choices you're making. There are good reasons to be working full time. Whether it's health-care insurance or that you actually enjoy your professional self or that your family needs the money. Those are legitimate, good reasons, and those are real-life lessons to your kids. Once you've made your decision, you need to keep moving forward. At the end of the day, you have to answer to yourself. Did I do my best work today? Was I a good parent today? Did I look my children in the eye today and acknowledge how they're feeling? But the guilt can make you crazy, and you need to at the end of the day say, 'Look at all the things I did accomplish,' instead of all the things I didn't accomplish. I think that we're a negative society, and you need to take a minute to say, 'Wow! You did great by your kids. You did great by your job. You managed a lot. That was a gift, and tomorrow you can do it again.'"

—Katharine, social worker, mother of two

When You Need Help

Maureen didn't have time for office politics or gossip. In fact, she avoided them like the plague. When she went to work she worked. It was more difficult than she thought it would be because the office was a small family management business—a larger environment would have allowed for more anonymity. Still, she worked hard to avoid the fray because she had a plan. It took her six years, not five as she had originally planned, but she accomplished the goal she had set for herself when she went back to work: to start her own business with the experience she would gain. She hung out her own shingle, opened her own firm, and started managing buildings, too. One of the strategies she credits for allowing her to reach that goal was that she constantly asked for help, and hired it when she was able to. She recommends that all working moms outsource whenever they can so they can focus on making money, or on their kids and family. It can get expensive, but some forms of help don't have to be unaffordable. And sometimes what seems expensive on the surface isn't so much when you factor in the value of the other things it allows you to accomplish or even enjoy. For example:

- Hire help to care for the kids, whether a nanny, day care, a babysitter, or after-school care.

- Get someone to clean your house if you can afford it.

- Have your dry cleaning delivered.

- Let the laundry pile up.

- Pay a kid in the neighborhood to mow the lawn or shovel snow.

- Try out concierge apps to deliver food and groceries or to run your errands.

- Order your groceries online to save time. Amazon.com's Prime Pantry is a great resource. Many local and national supermarket chains offer delivery, too.

- Try something like the Franklin Covey system of time management. I started using their products in my late twenties, and it's one of the only ways I could have simultaneously traveled for work, done a triathlon, started a new show, and written a book. It really helps you to keep yourself, your head, your heart, and your day on track.

- Drugstore.com can help, too, for health and hygiene products and other pharmacy needs.

- Have faith that your systems and support networks are working. You'll know soon enough if you need to adjust or make changes, but in the meantime, trust that you've done everything you can to ensure your family's security and happiness. You won't be able to give your all to your work life if you're always worried about what's going on at home.

Once you open up that mental space and keep your workday clear and free of distractions, you will kill it at work. Get ready to focus. Get the home to-do list off your desk and out of your mind and start rising in the ranks once again.

COMEBACK QUOTE

"One day, we were all talking about traffic and how burdensome it was for some of us, fighting it on the way in. And our vice president at that time said, 'Well, you guys can have flexible hours. You can just come in at ten and leave at eight if you want.' And certain people were like, 'Oh, great!' And I remember thinking, I can't drop my kid off at day care at ten and pick her up at eight. And when I

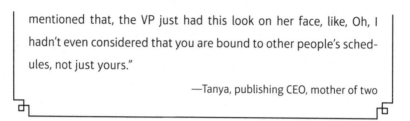

mentioned that, the VP just had this look on her face, like, Oh, I hadn't even considered that you are bound to other people's schedules, not just yours."

—Tanya, publishing CEO, mother of two

When You Have to Swallow Your Pride

Lori was a twenty-something Wall Street trader before she left the workforce in 1993 to have two children. As the kids became more self-sufficient, she decided it was time to go back to work. Her husband had his own business, so while they could definitely use her extra income, the more pressing need in those days before the Affordable Care Act was health insurance. Lori didn't want to go back to Wall Street hours or the New Jersey–New York City commute, so she searched for something new and more local. She found it in financial news, but the compromise didn't mean taking one step back, it meant taking three. She was hired in an entry-level capacity as a production assistant. She was starting from scratch at thirty-five years old.

Even though her job was printing scripts and organizing graphics for a TV network, she took her work as seriously as if she were running the place. Everybody in TV was young, but she had made a conscious decision not to try to fit in and act younger than she was. She would be ultraprofessional—the adult at the table who could tackle anything that came her way. (That's exactly what I did at KPIX. The other interns: smoking pot. Cheryl Casone the intern: making her résumé tape.) She maximized the skills that came along with life experience to overcome the technology curve and systems she needed to work on. She didn't talk much about her home life in the office because she quickly realized that that could alienate her from her younger colleagues. She did work hard to integrate and engage with her co-workers. She asked for help when she needed it and learned quickly.

While Lori initially seethed that she had been forced to take so many steps backward—something few men would ever do—she soon grew to appreciate the advantage it gave her. She wasn't competing against as many people to get in the door. She was able to tackle a new challenge almost risk-free, and find satisfaction and a certain amount of balance doing so. And she realized she was lucky that she had not waited any longer to get back in the game. Many of her friends were waiting until their kids were grown and out of the house to go back to work, but Lori's experience told her that in ten years, she would not have been able to take this career leap. She was still young enough to be engaged and energetic, and to fit in and feel young in a young crowd. If she had waited any longer, the entry-level position would have been off the table. Corporate America still needs to be able to see potential in you.

And clearly, corporate America did see something in Lori. Shortly into her new profession she was promoted. As the years went by, she continued to climb the corporate ladder. The pay scale was dramatically different from Wall Street's, but she was able to satisfy her success metrics:

- Earning an income? Check.

- Challenging career? Check.

- Health insurance for a family of four, and great benefits? Check.

- A job she could grow into and that fit into her fifteen-year plan? Check.

- An easy commute so she could still actively participate in her children's activities? Check.

What will your success metrics look like?

When You Face Bias or Discrimination

After a two-year break from a job on Wall Street, Eileen was ready to get back into the swing of things. Her plan, however, was to switch her sights from a megasized American bank to a smaller foreign one. Her headhunter assured her that the bank she was considering was touted as a kinder and gentler environment than the one she'd left, but with the same opportunities and income. Eileen hoped that would mean her bosses might be more tolerant of her occasional need to slip into mom mode. She also figured that a European bank would have earlier starting hours, which would still make for a long day but allow her to get home earlier to pick up her kids from school. Sure enough, after wowing the bank with her résumé and interview, she negotiated for a well-paid position that allowed her to leave at three or four in the afternoon and only had her in the office four days a week. So long as she met her ambitious financial projections, she could work her flex schedule. And her new office was located just blocks from her kids' school. Accepting the job was a no-brainer.

Though she missed taking the children to school in the mornings,

Eileen grew to love her job and her new role. One thing hadn't changed in the two years since she'd left, though: the industry was still cut-throat, and still stuck in an antiquated mind-set because it was dominated by men with stay-at-home wives who raised their kids and took care of all the details of their lives. Most of the people she worked with were nice, but her four-day week and the flex hours had some green with envy. After a few incidents where she had to run out early, and one individual's serious complaints, Eileen's boss came to her and said that while he respected her role as a mom, this was still a bank and the office couldn't handle the negative backlash and resentment stemming from her flexible-hours agreement. He told her she could stay, but she had to work the same hours as everybody else. Eileen was disappointed. Her performance was measured by how much money she generated, and she was meeting her goals, so the only reason to change her flexible schedule was because some people at the office just didn't like that she had one. Eileen was certain that whoever was objecting to her arrangement wasn't bothered by her supposed inability to stay focused at work, but didn't think she, a mom with young kids and a well-employed husband, should be there at all.

COMEBACK QUOTE

"When I came back to work briefly after my first child, my boss said, 'I'm shocked you came back. You have such a rich husband I didn't think we'd see you again.'"

–Alison, analyst, mother of two

Despite her disgust, Eileen decided to stay on, and enjoyed a highly successful tenure at the company.

The lesson? Moms have to do their jobs extremely well because they're judged through different lenses by their co-workers—and that goes double for any mom who arranges for a flexible schedule. Especially in certain traditional, male-dominated industries, the minute people find out you're a mom, you can be met with terrible bias. People might assume you're not committed or as tough. The same guys that will cut out early for a golf game will not hesitate to call you out for leaving early to watch your child perform in his class play. The same women who might take the occasional long lunch might look at you cross-eyed for doing the same so you can get your daughter to the orthodontist. Is their bias unfair? Yes. If you have concrete examples of discrimination in writing, and the situation is unbearable, you do have a case to bring to human resources. However, that should be your last resort. Next time you hear a joke like "Must be nice to have *your* schedule, must be nice to have that freedom" come back with a zinger like "Yeah, working off hours so I can wipe runny noses and do sing-alongs with fourth-graders is just great. Can I come play golf with you guys and drink beer please???" My friend has a saying for this style of communication: "be a nice bitch." You are getting a serious point across, but you are smiling when you do it. They'll get the message without it creating unnecessary workplace tension.

While it's not your responsibility to address people's biases against working mothers, you'll make life easier for yourself—and maybe help educate some people—if you take the following steps:

- Have a support system in place.

- Choose a good husband or partner because you're going to need them to step up and share the household responsibilities equally, and back you up when you have big projects or deadlines. You'll have a lot more strength to knock 'em dead at work if you know your husband will support your initiatives and be proud of your success.

- Don't act like a mom; nobody else cares about your kids.

- Don't let baby photos clutter your desk.

- At first, come in a little earlier than expected and put in the extra effort.

- Make one friend at the office who can cover for you or help you out in a jam, and be that person's backup, too.

- Keep your standards high—higher than most.

Several moms I spoke with told me that they felt discriminated against at work because of being a mom. Sometimes they weren't invited out to social gatherings with co-workers, other times they were passed over for assignments that required travel. Many felt they were constantly on the defensive, having to prove their worth in a way their male colleagues simply did not have to. As if because they had kids, they were incapable of prioritizing or figuring out how to juggle their roles as mothers and professionals. To hear them describe it, some industries haven't evolved much beyond what Patricia experienced back in 1974. She told me, "It was a different world altogether," but was it?

"Well, you had to prove yourself more than the men. [No man ever] said, 'Oh, I understand you have to take off work because your children are sick, or you have to take them to a doctor's appointment,' because they always had somebody else to do it for them. So you had to really be careful, because you wanted to keep your job. You had to be careful of how much you were out of work. You didn't want to have to run to school to pick up your kid because that would hold you back when it came to reviews. They'd always have that written down someplace."

Discrimination happens. You don't have to be a mom to experience it. I've been passed over for an on-air job because I didn't have the right "look" for a particular city, and I was told not to bother auditioning for a job because the people hiring were going "young." I was in my thirties. So old, right? It doesn't matter how many laws are on the books or how different things are for women now versus fifty years ago, at many companies, women, and especially moms, are still treated differently than men. They have to perform better to get the same promotions and the same pay. They have to go beyond the extra mile to prove their value to a company. The bias and discrimination are subtler than they were in the seventies and eighties, but they're still there, and they will continue to be as long as corporate America continues to be structured as though we were still living in the 1950s, without acknowledging the changing face and needs of the typical American worker. Things are much better now for working moms than they were for Patricia years ago, and improving daily, but we've got a long way to go.

Because bias and discrimination can still be problems, consider taking the following steps when beginning a new job:

- Get your agreement in writing. The e-mail chain can be an effective defense if you find yourself in an odd position. Always communicate with your boss, co-workers, clients, and others in writing. If you someday find yourself the victim of discrimination because you are a mom, you will need and want to have it all documented. Some lawyers say to keep a log. Keep it at home, not at work.

- Don't let them see you sweat. If you are starting to feel like you are being passed over for a promotion or assignment because you are a mom, don't express emotion or anger at work. Wait until you leave, and you can communicate your frustration in a safe place with your family or friends. Being labeled "unprofessional" will only hurt your image more.

- Do not leave one client call, e-mail, or project undone. When you make your case for a raise or promotion, make sure you have documented your successes and your strengths.

- Avoid topics such as religion, politics, sexual orientation, and health issues. Keep your head down.

- Know your rights. Be aware that discrimination in any form at work is illegal. No one can tell you "You have kids and can't make the dinner pitch meeting, so I'm giving the account to

Sally." That is open discrimination against you, and it has no place in the office. Period.

Of course, sometimes you're going to have zero interest in certain assignments, trips, sales dinners, and out-of-town client meetings. But you should always have the same opportunity to participate in them— or refuse them, if that's an option—as anyone else.

When It's Time to Move On

The first job you get isn't likely to be the last job you'll have. Nor should it be. It might be the hardest, but it will lay the groundwork for the next one, which could offer more money, better hours, or a better commute. It's the one you need to get the ball rolling to rebuild or start a new career and get closer to the salary you were once making in the years BC. Millennials job-hop, and whether or not you are one, unless you absolutely love your new job and it hits every one of your success metrics, you should, too. Get in, get the experience you need, and get out, especially if you're working a low-paying or part-time gig.

If you do find another job, don't fall into the trap of accepting a raise at your original company in exchange for staying. Recruiters will agree: the well is muddied once you tell an employer that you're leaving, even if you choose to stay on friendly terms. They know you were looking. Better to move on, take the higher wage elsewhere, and start fresh. The relationship with the current employer may never recover and memories are long: your lack of loyalty might make it easier for them to put *you* on the chopping block a year later instead of another employee.

Rising Above

No one thinks it's easy to overcome the challenges that working moms face, but the challenges are not insurmountable. Many of the stories in this chapter resonated with me because they highlight women who found ways to shine at work by finding a crack through which they could slip to make their mark. Look for the cracks you're not expecting to see, ladies—and then bust them wide open.

10

Work Smart, Not Just Hard

N obody is more efficient at work than moms, because they have two jobs—the one they're paid to do and the second one that starts once they get home. There's rarely time to linger at the watercooler or wait for other people to get it together. Once you go back to work, try to accomplish more in your eight to ten hours than everyone else. If you're driving the meetings, be militant about start and finish times. Block out your day at 8:01 a.m. when you get to your desk (already caffeinated and ready to start). Don't ease into the workday— you've already put in hours at home waking up the kids, so you're probably ready for action. Work smart, multitask, and get the job done.

One key to being able to engage at work and avoid procrastination is to love what you're doing. Jill is the chief accountant and operating officer for her family's business. She had a relatively smooth return to the workplace. Hers is staffed mostly by moms, so it's an understanding environment.

Jill developed her own formula, one that allows her to balance her commitment to family events and work, but even so, figuring out how to split up that time can be tough. She admits being in the family business allows her to put in fewer hours than she might at another job, but there's a trade-off there, especially for her ability to advance or expand her corporate options later. To compensate for the reduced time at work, she tries to be smart and efficient during her workday. Her advice to mothers out there trying to find a formula that works: There's no one way to do it. Everybody needs to evaluate their own personal situation and workplace and find what is right for them. There's no right or wrong way to finding your formula. The children will benefit both from seeing a mom at work, and from spending time with a mom who chooses not to. She says go with your own personal values and what feels right in your heart.

COMEBACK QUOTE

"It can be a very positive influence for children, plus working is an important piece of who I am. I really identify a big part of myself as not only Mom, but as a businesswoman who really enjoys the work that she does and the contribution that she makes."

—Jill, accountant, mother of one

CAREER EXPERTS SAY

"Working mothers . . . have an unbelievable way [of coming] into a work environment and [bringing] an ability to get to the essence of what is going on very quickly. When you are managing a lot, you have to be very focused. I think moms, because they're more balanced and have perspective, don't overthink things. You get into meetings with them, and they just have an unbelievable way of getting to what the root issue is. They just motor on, because they have a broader perspective and a broader life to get back to. So that is a huge thing. And I think the other thing is these moms have an ability

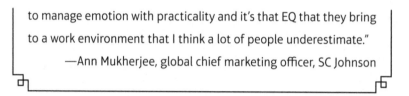

> to manage emotion with practicality and it's that EQ that they bring to a work environment that I think a lot of people underestimate."
> —Ann Mukherjee, global chief marketing officer, SC Johnson

Keep Your Head in the Game: Dealing with Office Distractions

The key to juggling family and being a success in the office is learning to *work smarter*, to not only be able to maximize time and quality of time spent at home, but also to maintain your place in the running for advancement and professional growth.

Everyone at work has to deal with distractions. There's the person who drops by your desk every morning to say hello. There's that client who calls every hour for an update on whatever project you're managing for them, and the *ping* from the computer that sounds off every single time you get a new e-mail. And of course there are all the distractions from your home life, like figuring out dinner for the whole week, or hoping your toddler doesn't catch the second-grader's stomach bug, and maybe even feeling guilty that you can't help serve cupcakes at the Valentine's Day party. I feel guilty if my cat, Milo, spends too much time alone; I can't imagine how moms feel if they're worried they're somehow shortchanging their kids.

Across the board, most moms say that the best way to reduce these distractions is to have a fully organized plan in place before you go back to the office. There's no winging it when it comes to food, child care, transportation, and extracurricular activities. Have not only a plan A in place but also a plan B:

- Who will you call if a pickup is needed?

- When will you get the groceries for the week and when will you be making lunches?

- Which neighbor's or relative's phone number do you have on speed dial in case of an issue?

Here's a list of solutions for ignoring time-sucking distractions so you can be efficient and smart with your time.

Don't be too connected. That *ping* that goes off for every new e-mail message that arrives in your in-box is annoying. First step, turn it off, then schedule a few times per day to go through those e-mails. It could be every hour, it could be every four. Find a rhythm that works for you. Same goes for your cell phone. Give explicit instructions to your child's caregiver or older child that they should call or text only in cases of emergency. Also, when you are in meetings, put that phone down and pay attention. Not only will you be more efficient, you'll have a leg up on the college grad who is savvy about technology, but deficient in life skills.

Create e-mail folders. In order to corral your e-mails, create specific folders to help you organize them so you make sure you eventually respond appropriately. You could organize them by project, sender, deadline, or order of importance. (I have one called "Comeback.")

Respond only when necessary. Don't waste your time or that of your colleagues by responding to an e-mailed question with "I'll let you know" or "I'll check." I know you're just trying to be polite, but all those little confirmation e-mails just add clutter and take time to read. Just check, and give an answer when you have one. Be specific in your headers and subjects and don't waste time cc'ing multiple people who don't need to be in on the conversation. Encourage that same behavior in your team. There's nothing worse than the obsessive cc'er.

Choose your watercooler time, and avoid Chatty Cathy. I've worked for many years in newsrooms, and many of us sit at blocks of desks that are open and visible to all. Several times I've sat next to people who do some distracting things that I simply can't stand like chew gum, eat loudly, talk on the phone loudly about nonwork issues, or talk to me about everything and anything that has absolutely nothing to do with work. It's not that I'm antisocial, but dealing with constant visitors to my desk (and now my office) can be a major distraction. This is where your mom patience can get you into trouble. Don't patiently listen to every bit of gossip or the details about someone's date, no matter how much you want to know. The time you spend listening to that is time you're not listening to your daughter tell you about her school play. Of course, you want to be polite, personable, and helpful, and try to bond with people, but be strict with the amount of time you spend talking casually to anyone around the office. The more time you spend with people, the less productive you are, and the less productive you are, the longer you may have to stay at the office, or take the work home. You can be patient with your kids, but don't be patient at work. It will distract you. If you're in a cubicle or at one of those massive shared tables that are in vogue now, you can use my old newsroom trick to protect yourself from that loud co-worker at the next desk or seat over: headphones. Many news producers wear headphones so the constant yelling from a breaking news event doesn't distract them. It helps!

Make a to-do list, then ignore it. I love lists. I make one for the grocery store, the household chores, and story pitches for the week. But sometimes those lists can hurt you, not help you, in the end. I always thought I was being überefficient with my Franklin Covey to-do list, and it is definitely a valuable organizational tool that I recommend, but I found myself recently checking it *too* often. I realized that my list could be a distraction if I obsessed about it. Find a balance. Lists are great, but it's counterproductive to focus on them too heavily. Besides, you'll get all sorts of things added to your agenda unexpectedly at the office that will throw your whole list off. Check it once or twice daily, but resist the urge to obsess about it.

Don't distract yourself. We are our own worst enemies, and this is true for most employees at major corporations. Whether it's checking Facebook during a break, or jumping from one task to another in the spirit of multitasking, American workers today have so many different balls in the air to juggle, it is inevitable that something—or everything—usually suffers. Don't let yourself fall into that trap. Don't let thoughts about the kids, your spouse, your commute home, and all the things you need to do this weekend slow you down. Block the same time off each day to make personal calls and set appointments. Setting a fixed time for dealing with your personal responsibilities will help you create structure in your work life, and that will reduce stress in your entire life.

You want to kick butt at work and kick back at home—to enjoy the dinner hour, you have to make it home for dinner. Leave when you're supposed to leave as your work is finished. Know what can wait and what must get completed. And don't let that to-do list pile up so that by Friday you're in a hole. Clear your plate as much as you can and get home to the good stuff.

You may find yourself floundering a bit at first, but with time, you'll figure out your new routines and tricks that will allow you to do your work in the time allotted. Will it be easier than sleep-training an infant? Or easier than juggling the schedules and needs of a bunch of small children? Not much, but at least your experience doing that lets you know you've got the smarts to figure out how to do what needs to be done in this new chapter of your life.

11

Making Progress and Paying It Forward

Some companies are starting to step up and recognize that it's to their advantage to create a welcoming environment for mothers. Jodie loved her job at Hasbro, where she'd spent fourteen years building a career, but by the time her twins turned six, she realized she was missing a lot, and they were noticing her absence. And when she was home, she was often working, on the phone, and not giving them her full attention. She was sad and conflicted, but knew she couldn't go all out at work and still go all out at home. The struggle was overwhelming. Moreover, when she looked around, she realized there weren't a lot of senior-level women doing it either, so she realized balance must not be possible. After some long and hard thinking, Jodie walked into human resources and quit her job at the company where she'd planned to work until she retired.

Hasbro, it turned out, loved Jodie too much to let her go. The CEO called her into his office and said, "We've got to make this work. What can we do, what can you do, so that you can stay with Hasbro?" He really valued her, and went out of his way to keep her. Jodie was floored. "Rather than letting me leave, they took it as an opportunity to say, 'How can we learn from this?'"

Jodie had worked her way up in the ranks and now the company, realizing her value, and that they employed a lot of other skilled mothers, wanted to make the environment better for working parents. Jodie was suddenly tasked with finding out more about the women at her company, reporting directly to the CEO and the head of HR.

After doing some research and critical thinking, she worked to create community networks and affinity groups at Hasbro. Suddenly, a very supportive environment formed at one of the oldest toy companies in the world.

"The skill these women demonstrate consistently is the ability to balance a crazy schedule, juggling priorities and giving their all to whatever commitment they've made. While they may be working full time, they're still managing the schedule of their family, and Hasbro has supported that in giving [them] flexibility. They've supported that by offering working from home if needed. We have a very supportive leadership team so that women or men, parents really, can ask for flexibility. It's a very supportive environment."

It was a win-win. The company needed mothers, not just for their work skills, but because they were the consumers of their products.

PowerToFly president Katharine Zaleski wrote an essay in *Fortune* magazine. She admitted that as a young woman in her twenties, she was unforgiving of her co-workers' leaving early to deal with child-care issues. Later, after she had a baby of her own, she said she looked back and was mortified. She would never have behaved that way had she known what it was like to have a child. She also knew that she still had a lot to offer corporate America, so she suddenly was on a mission to make space for moms.[21]

And then there's Doriana, whom we met in chapter 5. When she

---

21. Katharine Zaleski, "Female Company President: 'I'm Sorry to All the Mothers I Used to Work With,'" *Fortune*, http://fortune.com/2015/03/03/female-company-president-im-sorry-to-all-the-mothers-i-used-to-work-with/.

created a job-sharing opportunity at her company, she said that as a woman and a mom she tries to help create balance between home and life at work for women whenever she can. She helps them identify the shifts that work best for their schedules and remains sympathetic to their struggles.

These companies and individuals, among many others, are taking important steps toward making the working world an equitable place for moms. You can help. Once you get through the door, leave it open and help the next mom in any way you can. Until all companies recognize the value moms bring to the workforce, it will be your job to help others achieve success. That's what the hundreds of women who participated in this book did by speaking to me. They told me their fears, they shared their mistakes, and they explained their wins—all so that other moms could have an easier time making it than they did.

CAREER EXPERTS SAY

"There's a lot wrong with the workforce right now. Despite whatever policies might be on the books to protect working mothers, and we're certainly at a point where that's changing for the better, there's still a culture around work and what a good worker looks like that kind of comes out and bites working mothers and that just doesn't work in their favor. As much as we talk about flexibility, a lot of companies and a lot of managers really make assessments on performance based on very traditional models of what good work looks like. Moms don't necessarily fit those models."

—Rachael Ellison, organizational development consultant

and executive coach

What can you do?

- If you are struggling, speak to someone in HR, your boss, or whomever you are most confident with as you navigate this new reality of being a working mom. This goes back to my earlier point about having a friend who has your back when you are thinking about leaving on maternity. You always want to have an ally, someone you can trust to flesh out ideas or air grievances with first, before you decide to take any issues up the chain.

- If you've been able to negotiate a favorable arrangement, urge other moms to ask for one, too. This is called sisterhood, and it's one of the most important beliefs I hold as a woman who has been working since her teenage years. I always believe in the power of female relationships, and because women have yet to find parity with men on many levels, you should work to foster relationships with other women in the office, especially other mothers. Think of this as a "pay it forward" moment in your career.

- Help initiate leadership programs and assess ways to retain women with children, if you're in a position to do so. Think back to the story of Jodie at Hasbro. Her new position at the toy company was to help women, especially moms, see their potential and grow professionally and personally. It was initially her CEO's idea to change her role, but Jodie took that assignment and ran with it, making Hasbro one of the leading companies in the nation when it comes to empowering working parents, especially women.

- Research other companies with day-care options and see if there's a way to outsource services for mothers. Many large companies see the benefit of having day care or nursery care available inside the building, or they cover the cost to outsource the program. If your company doesn't have such a benefit, come up with a plan that you think may be financially feasible and present it to your HR contact.

Become a Mentor

Corporations today need moms for their skills, wisdom, and insights, but women are afraid to ask for what they need, especially when they're new to motherhood. They're still just trying to find their footing. It's up to the more experienced mothers to show them the way. Take the opportunity to educate others and be completely transparent with them about your struggles and daily challenges, and offer them strategies for balancing everything out. Being honest and transparent about the struggles really breaks down barriers and helps create a supportive team environment.

COMEBACK QUOTE

"We as women or moms, we don't speak up for what we need. If there is someone who inspires you or someone who's doing it well, who you aspire to be like, ask them. Ask them to have coffee. Ask them to have lunch. How did they do it? Lean on the senior women to help get you through so you can understand how to achieve balance, how you can further your career while still being a great mom. It doesn't have to be an either/or."

—Jodi, fitness instructor, entrepreneur, mother of two

We all need a mentor. Mine is Peter Shaplen. Before he was my mentor, he was my boss. I met Peter at my first job as a financial reporter for a start-up in San Francisco called ON24, and I remember Peter telling me that he couldn't pay me very much, but he'd be happy to coach me with regards to interviews, writing, editing, and on-camera delivery. Peter, our team, and I believed that video streaming on the Internet was the way of the future and that television would become obsolete one day. In a way we were right, we were just fifteen years ahead of it all. Netflix didn't exist. The dot-com bubble eventually burst, and we all moved on to other jobs. But the advice I gained from him has stuck. I still use it today, and whenever I'm struggling with an assignment, or just having a bad day, Peter is an e-mail or phone call away. Find yourself a Peter before you leave work, before you go into the search process, and once you land a gig.

At some point I became the mentor. Women need to work together. No matter how long I am lucky enough to work in the news business, I will look back with the satisfaction of knowing that I helped other young journalists (former interns, production assistants, and friends of friends) make their way into broadcast journalism. I took my cue from all the people who have helped me, from Peter to Neil Cavuto, who once listened to an intern's idea in a morning editorial meeting and made it the lead story for the show that day. "You never know where ideas will come from," he said. Wise words. Listen to everyone and be generous with your time. Make the mom mafia a thing in every place—there's power in numbers and room for everyone to succeed.

— CONCLUSION —

So many of the women I spoke with for this book told me that when they first decided to go back to work, they felt they had nothing to offer, nothing to give, and that corporations wouldn't value them. They found for the most part that the exact opposite was true, and that the multitasking, juggling, and child care that comes with stay-at-home motherhood amounted to the best training ever when dealing with cranky bosses, ungrateful clients, and immature co-workers.

One of the moms told me a story early on in my research that has stayed with me: It was her advice to moms, but it turned out to be great advice for me, too. She said, "I realized that my life as a professional, a mother, and a wife was the life of a juggler. I was constantly juggling several balls in the air at once, and I realized that at some point one of those balls was going to drop. And I had to learn that it was OK. A ball is going to drop. It's just the way it's going to be, this is reality."

I love that story. Whether you don't know if you want kids, or you are not sure if you want to work after having them, take that lesson with you. I think about her words every day, and it helps me to forgive myself if something falls through the cracks. You have to forgive yourself if you don't do it all. Balls will drop and that's OK. You are not superwoman, I am not superwoman, and if I meet a woman in

New York City who looks like she has it all, I remind myself she doesn't. Nobody is perfect.

Another favorite story: A mom told me she was sitting in her living room, and her triplets were screaming. Bloodcurdling screams, because it was lunchtime, and they were hungry. It happens, right? She was in the middle of working on her thesis for grad school, because for some reason she thought it would be a good idea to have small children and get her doctorate at the same time. (I mean who doesn't think that's a recipe for disaster?) So, she laid out a blanket on the living room floor, put all three babies on it, opened a box of cereal, dumped it on the blanket, and said, "Here, you guys, here's lunch." I almost fell off my chair laughing when she told me that story. Her kids are just fine, and she survived. You will, too.

— ACKNOWLEDGMENTS —

There are not enough words to thank the hundreds of women who took the time to be interviewed for this book. Your insights have been exceedingly helpful and will do some good in the world. It warmed my heart to find so many working mothers so eager to help other women and to share their time with me. There are so many of you who requested anonymity and there are so many to name, so I will just say with the utmost gratitude: you made this book what it is. You are all busy moms and yet you carved ten to twenty minutes out of your already painfully hectic day to be interviewed for this book: I thank you. I'm certain that the other moms out there coming up in the ranks or planning a return to work thank you, too. To the professional sources and executives who helped with this project: Stacey Delo, Carol Fishman Cohen, Katie Fogarty, Rachael Ellison, Jodie Neville, Sharon O'Connor, and Tom Gimbel. Thank you all for your time.

To you, the reader, I hope you find inspiration from the women featured in this book. I know they have inspired me more than I can express.

My writing partner in crime is Stephanie Krikorian, who might be the smartest, coolest chick I've met in my career as a journalist. Stephanie is practical, strong, and brave for working with me on this. It's been a long and crazy journey to get this book off the ground and then written, and she stuck by my side with honesty, smarts, and a "can do" attitude that kept me going, especially when I thought my dream of writing a book was impossible.

The folks at Portfolio/Penguin, Bria Sandford and Adrian Zackheim, took an enormous amount of time to help me formulate the concept for this project, fine-tune the idea, and get it just right. Your trust that I'd pull this book off was very much appreciated. Thanks for betting on me. Also at Penguin, Vivian Roberson and Stephanie Land.

To my agent of nearly a decade and a half, Laurie Jacoby at Napoli Management: You worked tirelessly to help me make the jump from San Francisco to New York and gave me hope by telling me repeatedly that "cream rises to the top."

To the people I work with and for at Fox News Channel and Fox Business Network:

Roger Ailes, Chairman and CEO, Fox News, for not just hiring me back in November of 2006, but for telling me to "stop sleeping with my phone and get a life." I took his advice. We all need a life, people to love, and a good night's sleep once in a while.

Dianne Brandi, executive vice president, legal and business affairs at Fox News. She might be the coolest and hippest lawyer, executive, and cheerleader I've worked with in my professional life. Her support and guidance through my time at Fox has been invaluable.

Gary Schreier, vice president of programming at Fox Business Network, for taking that meeting with the doughnuts and coffee at his office at Fox News before Fox Business was launched. If it wasn't for a frantic phone call one fall afternoon in 2006 from Gary, I wouldn't have gotten the interview with Roger Ailes. He changed my life.

Lauren Petterson and Jennifer Rauchet, two working moms at Fox News. They are incredible television producers, and they are two women who put the "manage" in management. It was their idea several years ago for me to start doing "On the Job Hunt" segments for *Fox & Friends*. The work on the show led me to write this book, and I'm forever grateful for your friendship.

To all the anchors past and present, in particular Gretchen Carlson, Elisabeth Hasselbeck, Steve Doocy, and Brian Kilmeade. You guys are the best part of going to work before the sun rises. My life is #betterwithfriends.

Clint Greenleaf. You are my spiritual leader when it comes to writing and publishing. You are also a great dad, and I have a feeling many moms out there would be lucky to have someone like you in their corner as they head back to the workforce.

To my family, who has supported me every step along the way. You never judged or criticized, and everyone needs that in their life! A big hug to my stepfather, Franz Zornes; stepmother, Susan Casone; my sister, Elizabeth Casone Ming; my brother, John Casone; and their spouses, Woei Ming and Maura Casone.

To my first and now closest friend here in the vast borough of Manhattan, Milissa Rehberger: you are a sister to me. If ever I need to bury a body, I know I can call you, and you'll bring the shovel.

To my dad, Joe Casone, who didn't live long enough to see me begin this book, but was always my biggest fan and watched all my shows, segments, and interviews on Fox News and Fox Business.

A special thanks to my inspiration and my personal "mom" hero: my mother, Marsha Zornes. She was the original working mom, and she set the bar pretty high. She also encouraged me to find a career that I loved, and work that I enjoyed, no matter what it was. She always told me, "I don't care what you do for a job, just do what you love."